BIZ KIDS GUIDE TO SUCCESS

Money-Making Ideas for Young Entrepreneurs

By Terri Thompson

Illustrated by Shannon Keegan

BARRON'S

Photo Credits
Chapter 1: Dan Abernathy
Chapter 2: Gerald L.Taylor
Chapter 3: Hassan Photography, Phoenix, AZ
Chapter 4: Acey Harper
Chapter 5: Hassan Photography, Phoenix, AZ
Chapter 6: Mike Scalf Photography, Inc.
Chapter 7: Gerald L.Taylor
Chapter 8: Jill LeVine
Chapter 9: Ed Hille

© Copyright 1992 by Barron's Educational Series, Inc.

All rights reserved.

No part of this book may be reproduced in any form, by photostat, microfilm, xerography, or any other means, or incorporated into any informational retrieval system, electronic or mechanical, without the written permission of the copyright owner.

All inquiries should be addressed to:
Barron's Educational Series, Inc.
250 Wireless Boulevard
Hauppauge, New York 11788

Library of Congress Catalog Card No. 91-40835

International Standard Book No. 0-8120-4831-8

Library of Congress Cataloging-in-Publication Data

Thompson, Terri.
    Biz kids' guide to success : money-making ideas for young
entrepreneurs / by Terri Thompson
        p.   cm.
    Summary: Discusses how young people can make money by
starting their own business.
    ISBN 0-8120-4831-8
    1. New business enterprises—Juvenile literature.   2. Small
business—Juvenile literature.   3. Entrepreneurship—Juvenile
literature. [1. Moneymaking projects.   2. Business enterprises.
3. Entrepreneurship.] I. Title.
HD62.5.T53 1992
650.1'2—dc20   91-40835
                                                                CIP
                                                                AC

PRINTED IN THE UNITED STATES OF AMERICA
2345   0100   987654321

TABLE OF CONTENTS

PREFACE

*This book is written for and dedicated to **biz kids**. What's a biz kid, you ask? That's the name I have given to any young entrepreneur (pronounced ON-trah-prah-noor) who uses his or her special interests, talents, and abilities to turn an idea into cash. Biz kids are inventive, creative, optimistic, and often funny. And they have learned how to juggle their work schedule around the demands of school and family.*

Within these pages you will read about some special and successful biz kids. Some are friends or relatives of mine; others are kids who came to my attention when their activities were featured in newspaper or magazine articles. Their stories are true experiences that I believe can show you ways to make money and have fun doing it.

Why be a biz kid? Money, of course, is one motive. But starting a business when you are young brings other rewards, too. For example, it may be a great help to you later when you are deciding what you want to be as an adult. Even kids who fail in their first few endeavors will learn from their mistakes. And those who are lucky enough to have a success right away will have made a tremendous leap toward financial independence and learning to take on the responsibilities of an adult career.

The important thing to remember when deciding how you want to earn money is that the work should be something you truly like to do. With the help of this book, you can pick an enterprise that is right for you. Then, talk it over with your parents to make sure it will not conflict with school or home commitments and you will be ready to begin.

*In reading this book, you will come across many new words (in **bold**). These terms appear in a glossary in the last chapter. You will also find many checklists and forms to guide you in your step-by-step business plans. I hope this book answers your basic business questions, and that you will keep it around for future reference as you and your new venture grow and flourish.*

CHAPTER 1

Kids as Entrepreneurs

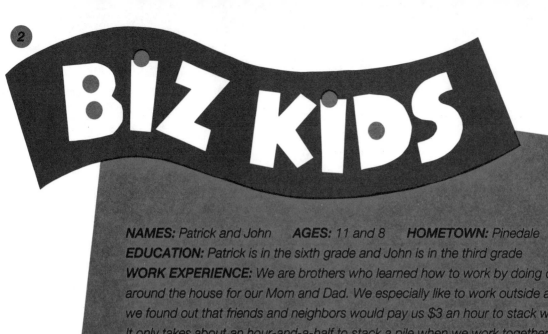

BIZ KIDS

NAMES: Patrick and John   **AGES:** 11 and 8   **HOMETOWN:** Pinedale

EDUCATION: Patrick is in the sixth grade and John is in the third grade

WORK EXPERIENCE: We are brothers who learned how to work by doing chores around the house for our Mom and Dad. We especially like to work outside and we found out that friends and neighbors would pay us $3 an hour to stack wood. It only takes about an hour-and-a-half to stack a pile when we work together, so we each get $4.50. That's pure profit because we have no costs.

PERSONAL: Patrick plays the violin and builds model airplanes and his favorite subject is drama. John plays the recorder, collects baseball cards, and wants to be a fighter pilot when he grows up.

MONEY GOAL: To make enough money to buy a dirt bike or snowmobile.

CHAPTER 1
Kids as Entrepreneurs

Meredith was in a pickle. Christmas was coming and she was out of cash to buy presents for her friends and family. The energetic and ambitious eleven-year-old already did chores around the house to earn a $3-a-week allowance. But, with the cost of everything from school supplies to movie tickets constantly rising, that money was spent almost before it reached her pocket. Most of her money went for paints, brushes, and canvases, the tools of her favorite pastime—painting. She hated to ask her parents for a raise. She knew that grown-ups' money is limited, too.

Then it hit her. Meredith could put her artistic talent to work to earn extra cash. After all, her Mom's friends admired Meredith's vivid oil paintings and offered to <u>pay</u> for them. To Meredith, painting was a hobby—something fun to do. But other people saw value in her art and would spend $20 for a "Meredith original." Soon, Meredith was rolling in **profits** from her paintings.

Does Meredith's predicament sound familiar? Does the week almost always outlast your allowance? Do you find yourself short on cash just when the best sales are on at the shopping mall? With college costs skyrocketing, you may want to start **saving** now to afford a good education. These are common reasons for being interested in money.

Resolving a money problem takes a little ingenuity. But for enterprising kids, there is a solution. Rather than asking their parents for money and getting another "money-doesn't-grow-on-trees" lecture, a lot of smart and industrious kids are starting up their own money-making businesses. They are what the business world calls **entrepreneurs**—people so sure they can make a profit that they take risks to prove it.

Sound scary? Well, it can be, especially if your business idea requires a big **investment**. But, if you are like most "biz kids," the major investment will be your precious time—after school, weekends, and even during vacations—and the most important ingredients for success will be drive, determination, and discipline. Of course, you also have to have a good **service** or **product** to sell—something people will spend their hard-earned money on. And figuring out which product or service to offer is hard work, too. But Meredith and thousands of kids like her have proven it can be done.

Basically, the secret to success is to watch for things people do not have time to do for themselves. Busy people need lots of help—from grocery shopping to housecleaning. Kids can run errands, wash cars or windows, polish shoes, mow lawns, shovel snow, walk dogs. Mothers with toddlers always need babysitters. You can get started working for relatives and friends of the family; if you are reliable, word will spread about your skills and abilities.

The good thing about these service businesses is that they do not cost a lot . Your biggest **expense** may be cards and posters that advertise your availability to serve. But be realistic about what you can do and will enjoy doing. For example, if you really do not like little kids, don't go into the babysitting business. Likewise, if dogs make you sneeze, a pet grooming or walking service isn't for you.

Before picking his business, ten-year-old Brandon put a lot of thought into it. At first he considered offering a wake-up service, since his family already owned the necessary equipment: an alarm clock and a phone. But when the Miami youngster thought about the awesome responsibility of getting up early himself to make those all-important phone calls, he decided it wasn't such a good idea after all. In the end, Brandon chose to start a flower delivery service, which he called "Bloomin' Express." He charged clients about $20 a month to deliver a fresh bouquet of flowers every week. Brandon got the idea when he noticed that flowers sold at a local supermarket wilted after just a day or so while posies his Mom bought from a **wholesaler** remained fresh all week. He talked to neighborhood moms who assured him they would pay for the quality and convenience of his home delivery service. So he bought flowers from a wholesaler and charged twice his cost. After six months in business, Brandon had profits of $75 a month.

SPECIAL TALENT Earning money by using a special talent or hobby is like getting paid for having fun. For example, kids with a flare for the dramatic can put their creative skill to work by putting on magic shows for parties or delivering singing messages. Vincent, a Manhattan high schooler and aspiring musician, got paid to write and record his own positive rap songs like "Drugs No Good" ("Your body's very delicate/It can't take no crack/Crack or no smoke or no dope or no coke.")

Artistic kids can make crafts for holiday gifts. Nicole, a fourteen-year-old from Buford, Georgia, used calligraphy to do ornamental ink lettering on party invitations and poems on parchment paper. In Douglaston, New York, thirteen-year-old David put his experience with computers and graphics programs to work by starting his own greeting-card and sign-making business. He sold his cards for fifty cents apiece. During the holidays he pulled in about $100 in a two- or three-week period. Jana and Michelle of Humble, Texas, were good at wrapping gifts. One Saturday before Christmas these ambitious twelve-year-olds asked the manager of a pharmacy if they could set up a gift-wrapping table in the store. The manager thought it was a terrific idea and he provided the supplies. The girls had fun, and in one afternoon each earned $15— just in time for Christmas.

SPOTTING OPPORTUNITY What do all these biz kids have in common? They found a product or service people wanted, and they sold it. For example, one weekend, Duane of Sugar Land, Texas, noticed that everyone at the local swim meet seemed thirsty. The next weekend he made $50 selling snow cones. Emily set up her food-and-drink stand where many people passed by on their way to a nearby yacht club. She charges a little less than stores, and she still earns more than twice what she spends to make her brownies and lemonade.

Other kids have spotted the "thirst-and-hunger" **market** and adopted their own variations of the old-fashioned lemonade stand. Kim and Mike found that soft drinks sold better than lemonade, while Chris had a booming business selling Kool-aid.® Some kids sell Popsicles® and home-baked goodies or sandwiches as well. For extra cash, you may even be able to provide a special service.

Sisters Ann and Jenny of St. Paul, Minnesota, for example, made $35 a day standing on the edge of a golf course near home, selling canned drinks to thirsty golfers. In addition, they got extra tips for chasing balls that went over the fence.

*With all the **competition**, sometimes you have to come up with a gimmick. Ashley and Karsten invented a plan guaranteed to draw attention to their homemade chocolate chip cookies. They sang. In less than half an hour, these boys sold six dozen cookies and made $17 by singing their **sales pitch.***

*Sometimes even the smallest food-and-drink establishments can turn into big enterprises. At age thirteen, Brian set up a portable barbecue pit in the parking lot of his grandmother's grocery store. He cooked and sold hamburgers during the summer. The next year, "Brian Burgers" became an official business with health department permits and a bright red trailer and grill. Kenneth, of Gary, Indiana, started a small catering business at age sixteen. Now, just a few years later, he **employs** twenty-five teenagers and five adult cooks. All it takes, he says, is time, self-confidence, and determination.*

CONFIDENCE   Owning his own business has given sixteen-year-old Andrew of Milwaukee, Wisconsin, what he calls "a wonderful sense of achievement and confidence." He dreamed up his designer T-shirt business, "Candyland Creations," after he saw his favorite rock group, the Grateful Dead, in concert. Anyone who ever saw the "Dead" in action knows about their brightly colored psychedelic T-shirts. They look like tie-dyed remnants of the '60s generation. Well, when Andrew saw how Dead fans still snapped up these tie-dyed numbers, he knew he had a great idea. Today he works three hours a day making large orders of tie-dyed Tees, which sell for $9 each to two large department stores as well as to individuals. He has branched out into silk-screening, and designs T-shirts for high school volleyball and basketball teams. Andrew plans to study business in college. His long-term **goal** is to own a clothing store chain.

Fashion is definitely a big teenager business. Sean, now eighteen, earned $6,000 during two summers on Cape Cod streets peddling jewelry made of shells to what he called "blue-haired ladies who visit on tour buses." And Kevin, of Loudonville, New York, sells popular day-glo neon bracelets at ski slopes. But, as Andrew attests, the biggest money-making fashion tends to be designer T-shirts. Now a freshman at the University of Nebraska, Kelly started selling T-shirts at sixteen. He operated his booming business, "Koala Tee Inc.," from his parents' home in Omaha, Nebraska. Adam, of Denver, Colorado, started even earlier. At twelve, he decorated a shirt for his mother. She wore the shirt to work, others wanted one like it and the next thing Adam knew he was in business. Gerald, a Philadelphia high-schooler, plans to come out with a line of silk-screened T-shirts and designer sportswear called "Slam Dunk Fashions." The six-foot-nine-inch entrepreneur knows something about the business: he's a star basketball player.

GAMES   It helps to know something about the product you want to sell. But fashion is by no means the only commodity at which kids are experts. They are especially good at inventing games, and some even make money at it. Michelle, a twelve-year-old girl from Fresno,

California, created a board game of international relations and conflict resolution called "Give Peace a Chance," for which she received the International Peace Prize. Kids from 150 countries have played it, and she set up Peace Works, Inc., to manufacture and market her game. Another twelve-year-old, Hannah, of Hollywood, California, invented a game called "Cardz" that is like cards and Scrabble® rolled into one. And Brian, fourteen, of Corpus Christi, Texas, makes miniature ramps for finger-sized skateboards of scrap plywood and cardboard. He sells them for $3 and up to friends at school.

ADULT APPEAL   Products that appeal to grown-ups are likely to be even bigger successes since those are the **customers** with the deepest pockets. Refrigerator magnets proved an enormously popular item for Dan of Los Osos, California. At twelve, he produced a magnet in the form of a small sea gull perched on a rope-bound piling. Four years later he was producing nearly 50 different refrigerator magnets and other decorative woodcrafts and gifts. Orders for his products came from across the country, including Disneyland, Disneyworld, Knott's Berry Farm, and a chain of Hallmark stores.

COMPUTERS   The computer age is a bonanza for computer-literate kids. With her desktop publishing service, thirteen-year-old Wendy of Lincoln, Rhode Island, produced **newsletters**, **fliers,** and **brochures** for friends and relatives. She also published a newsletter five times a year called <u>Wendy's Gazette</u>. Alexander, an eighth grader in North Miami Beach, Florida, specialized in personalized greeting cards, invitations, banners, and order forms. Calling his business, appropriately enough, "Computer Art To Go," he did all his work on a computer and computer-printer. He already owned a computer and software so his only costs were inexpensive paper and printer ribbon. Clients could order, if he was not home, *by leaving a message on his Mom's telephone answering machine. Alexander realized that if his business did well, he'd need his own phone and answering machine.*

PETS *For animal lovers, there are plenty of pet-related business opportunities. Mari earned $25 a day showing other people's dogs at dog shows. Scott gave dog-obedience lessons after school when his homework was done and customers were home from work. Other kids pet-sit for vacationing pet owners. If you are a good photographer, consider selling framed pet photos. Other specialty items for pets are designer collars, unusual toys, healthy doggie treats, or grooming aids.*

BABYSITTING *Babysitting is a big business—particularly with the growing population of working mothers. A difficult task is figuring out what to charge for this important service. Kate did her research by asking her friends what they charged. Some made $2.50 an hour, so she started by asking for $2. She got that all-important first job, and then she got lots of calls and charged more than $2.50. Mike of Washington, D.C., said he visited a family before he would agree to babysit. First he asked to see the kids and then he let them show him around the house. Meeting the family helped him feel confident enough to talk about money. Finding out what the job involves helps you decide what to charge.*

TUTORING *Kids who enjoy working with other kids are not limited to babysitting, of course. Wendell, a Leesville, Louisiana, high school student with a 4.0 grade average, started a tutoring business, instructing students in reading and learning and study skills. He tutored kids in English, math, science, and social studies and also helped prepare students for the SATs. Originally, he relied on referrals to promote his business, but then he distributed fliers at schools and was **recommended** by various faculty members. His business was so successful he is now **expanding** by hiring other qualified tutors to work for him. In addition to earning money,*

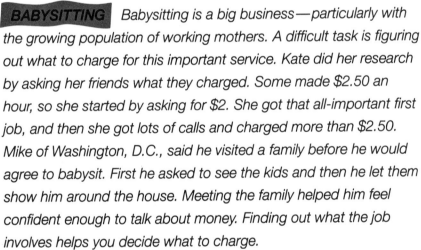

Wendell takes a lot of pleasure and pride in helping fellow students with learning disabilities.

BUSINESS REWARDS *To be sure, money is not the only thing gained in running your own business. Think of the other rewards: the knowledge gained, challenges met, obstacles overcome, and the sheer satisfaction from doing it on your own. And, the more you want to succeed, the better you will do.* **Entrepreneurship**, *of course, is not for everyone. If you do not take responsibility for yourself—say it takes hours of nagging from your parents or a teacher to motivate you to do your homework—you may have to forget about it. You probably do not have the drive and determination a successful entrepreneur needs. On the other hand, if you are a self-starter with bulldog tenacity and a good imagination, a small business may be your ticket to an early success leading to even bigger successes.*

CHAPTER 2

Tools of the Trade

BIZ KIDS

NAME: Robin   **AGE:** 12   **HOMETOWN:** Kingman

EDUCATION: Currently in the seventh grade

WORK EXPERIENCE: I run a lemonade stand in my front yard during summer vacation and sometimes on weekends. I make the lemonade myself, usually with fresh lemons that I purchase on sale from the grocery store. Otherwise, I have to use frozen concentrate, which doesn't taste as good. My costs are 25 cents for a small glass. I charge 30 cents, which means my profit is 5 cents per glass. I advertise with a big, bright yellow sign that people can read from across the street.

PERSONAL: I like to bowl. My hobby is collecting clowns. I belong to Awana, a church youth group, and I'm a member of the I Care Club for good citizenship. My favorite subject is English.

CAREER GOAL: To work in a pet store.

CHAPTER 2
Tools of the Trade

f you are still reading this book, then chances are you have already taken the first step toward entrepreneurship: you are thinking about running your own money-making business. The next step may be the most crucial one: convincing Mom and Dad you have a good business idea and you've got what it takes to make it work.

For that to happen, you have to prove you have stick-to-itiveness as well as a head for business. You need to learn the language of business so you can tell your folks how much profit you think you can make and where you expect to find a market for your product or service. The more knowledge you show, the more convinced they will be you can handle it. Picking a business that is right for you takes planning and plenty of research, but learning the basic tools of the trade is relatively easy.

Have you ever tried to run a lemonade stand? If so, you already have some idea of how a business works. Now, let's put it into the language of business.

To begin with, you had to buy all the stuff to make the lemonade—sugar, lemons, and paper cups. In business, the ingredients of a product are called **raw materials**. What those raw materials cost are your expenses. The lemonade, when it is ready for sale, is your **finished goods**. And the money from the sale of the lemonade is your **income**. If you were smart or lucky, you sold all your lemonade for more money than the raw materials cost, and you had a profit. That is, your <u>in</u>come was more than your <u>out</u>go. If, on the other hand, your **outgo** (expenses) were greater than your income, you had a **loss**. Losses mean your price was too low to cover all your costs. Or perhaps your price was too high and you could not get enough people to buy because they could buy it elsewhere for less money.

SUPPLY AND DEMAND In the United States and many other democratic countries, we operate in a <u>free market</u> **economy**. That doesn't mean everything is free. It means the price of everything is set by buyers and sellers who are free to participate in the economy.

If there is a shortage of something people want, they may be willing to pay more for it, and that pushes up the price everyone pays. The reverse is also true. If there is too much of some product, the sellers will lower the price to persuade people to buy it.

This is what is known in the business world as <u>supply and demand</u>. Generally speaking, too much **supply** of a product or too little **demand** from **consumers** pushes down the price a buyer pays. The flip side is that too little supply or too much demand makes buyers willing to pay more for something. What determines a product's price is the number of sellers and the amount they're selling and the number of potential buyers and how much they need of what is offered. At your lemonade stand, if someone opens a stand directly across the street and sells lemonade as good as yours for less money you have to charge less.

Estimating your income and expenses before you start a job or business helps you set your prices high enough to make a profit. It also helps you avoid the mistake of starting something that will not make enough money. Now you need to know the four basic building blocks of business: accounting, management, marketing, and finance.

ACCOUNTING To operate any business, whether it is a lemonade stand, delivering newspapers, waxing cars, or running a company like IBM, you have to keep track of what is being spent and what is being earned. This process is called **accounting**, which means keeping a written record of all financial transactions. Why go to this trouble? Because there is no way to tell whether or not you are making or losing money unless you put it down in black and white.

At your lemonade stand, let's say you list your raw materials and their cost. At the end of the first month, you discover the lemons cost $100, the sugar cost $30, and the paper cups cost $25. But you also spent $10 on a yard sign, $25 on advertising fliers, and $30 on a pitcher. Add that up and you find that your total expenses for the month were $220.

Now calculate the income side of the ledger. During the first week you sold 50 cups; the second week you sold 75 cups; the third week you sold 100 cups; and the fourth week you sold 125 cups. Total cups of lemonade sold = 350. You charged 50 cents for each cup of lemonade. So, you had a total income of 350 x 50 cents or $175.

Wow! That $175 seems like a lot. But your **bookkeeping** records show that your income does not even match your expenses. In this month alone you lost $45.

Is it time to give up? Not necessarily. First of all, you might consider raising your price. If you charged 70 cents instead of 50 cents per cup, you would have earned 350 x 70 cents or $245—for a nice profit of $25. Here is how that is calculated: $245 (income) minus $220 (expenses) = $25 (profit). That assumes, of course, that people would have been just as eager to buy your lemonade even though it cost 20 cents more. The risk is that you might lose customers who did not think your lemonade was worth that much.

But even if you do not raise your price, you are bound to make more profit in the second month than in the first month. Can you see why? Because some of those costs will never be repeated. For example, you will not need a new yard sign and you will not need another pitcher—unless you break it. And you may decide that the advertising flyers aren't necessary, so you can save another $25 there. Without these costs and assuming the same number of customers, you will have a profit in the second month of $20: $175 (income) minus $155 (expenses) equals $20 (profit).

Obviously, if you spend $220 in order to earn $175, you are not doing very well. But, without a written record, you might never know for sure. Of course, not only do you have to keep detailed records of your costs and income, you also have to prepare tax returns for federal, state, and local governments. For that reason, in particular, you should organize your business records in an orderly way and keep track of the health of your business with records that size up your financial progress over time. Chapter Four teaches simple bookkeeping and accounting guidelines.

MANAGEMENT   *In business, **management** means leadership. As the manager of a business, your tasks are to **plan**, analyze, control, and organize. You may know how to do some of these jobs already without realizing it. You can learn more as you read on and find out what is involved. Management is being the boss and carrying total responsibility. You control your business destiny—whether it succeeds or fails.*

MARKETING   ***Marketing** is perhaps the most important function in a new business. It means getting the right goods and services to the right people at the right price, at the right time and place, with the right advertising and promotion. How do you figure out what is right? Put yourself in your customer's position and look at your business from the customer's point of view. Keep in mind:*

THE CUSTOMER IS ALWAYS RIGHT!

Is your lemonade the best tasting in town? Or is it too sweet? Too sour? To find out, just ask your customers. What do your customers want and how do you let them know you can give them what they want? As a marketer you design the best possible product or service that will meet your customer's needs, set a price high enough to earn a decent profit but low enough to attract customers, and, finally, promote yourself by letting people know you're in business.

Good marketing makes people want to buy your products. The best marketing methods depend upon your business and budget and where your customers are. For example, you might advertise your lemonade stand with posters on utility poles at either end of your block. It is cheap and effective—especially if you are selling something cool and refreshing on a hot summer day. For more on marketing your business, read Chapter Six.

FINANCE   *Finally, you have to know something about **finance**. This is the realm of money and banking. You probably already know how to make change so if someone gives you a dollar bill for a 70-cent cup of lemonade, you know to give him or her back 30 cents. If you do not know how to make change, learn by practicing with* your Mom or Dad or someone who can make sure you are correct.

Most kid-sized ventures do not need a lot of money to start—what's known in the world of high finance as **start-up capital**. And, in the early stages of your business, you may be able to stash the proceeds in a shoebox or piggy bank. Eventually, however, you probably will handle larger sums of money and, at the very least, should open a savings or checking account with a local banker. In Chapter Five, you'll learn more about money and banking.

GOALS AND BUDGETS One of the things you can do now is to make a money plan or **budget**. Think about your own personal goals. Why do you want to make money and how are you going to spend it? To buy something specific, like a bike or CD-player? To save for college? To go to the movies once a week? Then, how much money can you earn? Your answers to these questions will change as your goals change and your income grows. As you set new goals, write a new budget. List all your income (how much you will get) and your expenses (how you want to spend the money).

It is easy to see that your income must be enough to cover the amount you plan to spend. If it isn't, you have a problem. Either you have to earn more or spend less. This is called **balancing the budget**. If you have trouble balancing your budget, be realistic. List what you need or want in order of importance; the things at the bottom of the list will have to wait until you have more money.

Also, be realistic about how much money you can make. Do some research. Use the library or talk to people who know about the product or service you want to sell. Check out the competition, too. How many others are in the area you want to cover? If you are lucky, you may find few or none. What do they give for what they charge? If you want to succeed, you must be able to offer a better deal: more or better service for less money.

Think about when you will work and where you will get customers. Do trial marketing. Check with neighbors and friends about their willingness to buy your service. Talk with your parents about your money-making idea and ask them for suggestions.

Impress them with your understanding of the importance of planning, and they may have good ideas to help you reach your goals.

Selling a product or a service means selling yourself to customers—convincing them that you are **dependable** and responsible. But first you have to prove to your parents that you are all that…and more. For example, you may have to show that your business idea can be scheduled around school activities, family obligations, and your household chores.

You benefit from running your own company: It introduces you to business basics. It teaches you first-hand how the business world works. Most important, it gives you experience you can use to get a job, to gain admission to the college of your choice, or to start a **career** that could last a lifetime. Your parents will be pleased you are learning the value of work and money. In fact, they shouldn't object at all to your money-making plans.

Now that you know about the basic "tools of the trade," it is time to put that knowledge to work. If you have not selected a business **venture**, read on. Chapter Three is full of ideas to start the wheels turning in your new-found business brain.

EXPENSES		INCOME	
lemons	$100.	50 cups, week one	$25
sugar	30.	75 cups, week two	$37.50
paper cups	25.	100 cups, week three	50.
yard sign	10.	125 cups, week four	62.50
flyers	25.	TOTAL	$175.
pitcher	30.		
TOTAL	$220.		

CHAPTER 3

Choosing a Business Venture

BIZ KIDS

NAME: *John*   **AGE:** *10*   **HOMETOWN:** *Phoenix*

EDUCATION: *Currently in the fifth grade*

WORK EXPERIENCE: *Pet-walker. I like to be outdoors, and dogs seem to like me. I charge $2 to walk a dog for 15 minutes; $4 for half an hour. To make more money, I sometimes walk more than one dog at a time. I get business from my neighbors and by going door-to-door. I will do any outdoor chore, such as mow lawns or take out trash. I also like to work with friends. Sometimes we wash cars as a team. I keep track of the money I make in a spiral notebook.*

PERSONAL: *My favorite subject is math. I play on my school football team and collect football cards.*

GOAL: *I want to attend Notre Dame on a football scholarship.*

CHAPTER 3
Choosing a Business Venture

If you have not set a goal for yourself or picked the business of your dreams, do not be discouraged. Instead, do some soul searching. Appreciate your own money-making abilities. Make a long list of your talents and skills and list your interests. Do not worry if your talents-and-skills list is not as long as your interests list. You can always learn new skills to match your interests. Right?

IMAGINE THIS Now for the fun part. Turn your imagination loose. Do you have a favorite craft you are good at? Perhaps you could produce these items and sell them or teach others your craft. Do you enjoy wrapping gifts or is your handwriting neat? At holiday times, in particular, wrapping gifts and addressing cards are excellent ways to make money. Do you like to take photographs with your camera? Think about taking snapshots for a fee. If you like the outdoors, consider a complete yard care service: mowing in the summer, raking in the fall, shoveling snow in winter.

You will have the greatest success working at what you like. Select a business that fits your personality. If you are shy or like working by yourself quietly, you might clean houses or wash windows. If you are a ham at heart, why not deliver singing telegrams or be a birthday party clown.

Do not set yourself up in something you know you will hate. If you detest piano playing—even if you are good at it—do not teach piano. No matter the demand, if you do not like playing the piano, you will not be a good teacher, and you will not stick with it long.

Selecting a business that is right for your community is another important step. Look around to see what needs to be done. Talk to your neighbors or give them a questionnaire. Seeing opportunity is the first part of success. Doing something about it is the second part, and it takes both parts to reach a goal.

Most kid ventures today are "service" businesses. That means you sell your time, energy, and expertise to perform tasks for others. Usually, these are jobs people hate or do not have the time or energy to do. Things like cleaning and lawn-care are dandy service businesses. The other type of business is "product-oriented."

Are you a born salesperson? Then you may prefer a product-oriented business in which you make or buy your products and sell them **door-to-door***, from a booth in your front yard, or at school.*

If you want to sell services—rather than a product—think first about whether you would like to work outdoors or indoors, with younger children, older adults, or pets. Or can you use a hidden talent? Find a service that needs to be done and matches your skills and desires. Here are some ideas:

YOU WANT TO WORK OUTDOORS? *How about a complete lawn-care and landscape service? You can weed and water yards, mow lawns, rake leaves, plant flowerbeds or small bushes, trim hedges, and do edging. Know how to operate all yard tools properly before you begin. Ask your parents if you can practice on your backyard. You can get regular work by being polite and setting an appointment for next time. Clean up afterwards by sweeping walks and driveways and bagging clippings or trash. If you are responsible and good at your work, word-of-mouth will bring you plenty of customers.*

Look around your neighborhood for fences, sheds, dog houses, garages, or lawn furniture that need painting. Leave an announcement or flier describing your painting service at homes that need work. Your customer will probably supply the paint, but you may need brushes, rollers, rags, and other supplies. When you work, wear old clothes, shoes, and a cap, and cover surfaces that are not to be painted. Before you begin, remove mud, dirt, or loose paint with a dry brush or paint scraper. Then, paint with an up and down stroke, from top to bottom. Be neat, and clean up any mess.

FRIENDLY FUN *Washing and waxing cars can be fun with friends if you use an assembly line. Each of you can clean a certain car part, from the headlights and windows to the fenders and bumpers. Bring car wax and cleaning materials, rags and buckets, and have access to running water. Figure on at least two hours or more for each car, and set a flat* **fee** *for each you wash. To introduce*

your service to new customers, offer to clean the inside free. Then, when they see what a great job you do, you will have a steady client.

If you live in an urban area, consider an errand-running service. Errands include going to the post office or the store or dry cleaners, delivering packages, returning a book to the library, or buying a newspaper. Understand exactly what your customer wants before you leave, and write it down. Get a list of addresses and special instructions—also in writing—and be quick. Come straight back, and carefully deliver the items in good shape. The more reliable you are, the better your chances of being called on again.

There is even work to be found in golfing, and being a caddie is not hard. Mostly you carry golf clubs for, on average, $20 per round. If you play golf or understand the game, you have a head start. Otherwise, get books from the library or learn from observing. Contact any golfers you know and offer to caddie at a reduced rate for experience. Watch what other caddies do and ask questions. Leave your name and phone number at the golf course and wait for the calls to pour in.

If you live in a snowy place , a lucrative outdoor winter business is snow-shoveling. People will depend on you to clear their walks or driveways the minute it stops snowing, so it is important to deliver prompt service. That may mean getting up early so your neighbor can pull out of the garage by 8 A.M. You can advertise to small businesses or schools in your area. For guaranteed business, sign a winter-long contract. Then, hope for the white stuff.

As you can see, there are plenty of outdoor jobs . All you have to do is look. Taking people's trash cans to the curb and back on collection day is another way to earn cash. Running a shoe-shine stand in your neighborhood or a route to collect shoes and return them polished could be a steady business.

YOU PREFER TO WORK INDOORS? There are probably even more indoor jobs than jobs done out-of-doors, but they may not be as easy to spot, simply because you cannot see them. For example, you are not likely to see the dishes in your neighbor's sink or the

dirty laundry heaped in the basement. However, you have to think about the jobs at your house and remind yourself that all households require work.

With this in mind, you consider hiring yourself out as a mother's helper. You could dust, mop, sweep, vacuum, wash dishes, polish silverware, and mend clothing or sew on buttons. If you are a naturally tidy person who loves to organize, you could sort things out and put, for example, books, tapes, videos, or even spices, into alphabetical order. You can organize kitchen cupboards, the garage, or the basement workshop. Distribute fliers around your neighborhood and see what interesting jobs come your way.

Cleaning is never-ending. And that is good news for you if you have a cleaning service. From cat litter boxes to bathrooms, kitchens, basements, and attics, you can offer a super-duper service of floor-to-ceiling cleaning. Since no particular skills are required, getting started is easy. Begin by offering your service to friends and relatives. Word of mouth gets you more customers if you do good work. Since expectations vary from job to job, find out what each customer wants—specifically. Ask for detailed instructions of what needs to be done and check the items off a list as you do them. Be careful with cleaning solutions and do not damage property; you may be held responsible and have to pay for mistakes. If the customer does not supply the cleaning materials you need, make sure you have them and can transport them to the job. You will most likely charge an hourly rate for your service; of course, you have to charge more if you are supplying the cleaning solutions as well as elbow grease. Inspect your work before you say you are finished. Keep a list of customers and contact them regularly. At some point, you can expand your business to washing windows, barbecues, fireplaces, or pools. Let your regular clients know about your new-and-improved services.

As you may know, many people like to have their clothes washed and ironed, but they hate doing it themselves. You can provide a laundry service. Have your customers drop off their dirty clothes and linens and, at a specified time, pick them up.

Alternatively, you can offer to do wash in your customer's home. This business will require use of a washing machine and dryer, ironing board and iron, and you have to learn the proper way to press clothes. Be very careful, because if you ruin a garment, you will have to replace it. It is best to charge by the piece, rather than the hour. And you must be able to complete the job when promised it or you will quickly lose customers.

When people go on vacation, they can use the services of a house-sitter. You do not have to actually stay in the vacant house. What you can offer is to check on the house while empty, pick up mail and newspapers, water indoor plants, feed pets, and turn lights on at night.

These are just a few examples of indoor jobs. Can you think of others?

DO YOU LIKE BEING AROUND YOUNG CHILDREN? *If so, consider being a babysitter. Babysitting is not for everyone. You need to be at least ten years old, trustworthy, know how to care for kids, and—most important of all—to really enjoy being around babies or little children. There is always the standard method of babysitting, where you go to the child's home. Dependable sitters can become very popular, but minding just one child at a time can be a slow way to make money.*

You can multiply your earning power by taking care of several children at once. For example, you and a friend can have a "latchkey" service, watching up to six school-age children in your home after school until their parents get off work. Or, you can offer a regular time, say Saturday or Sunday afternoon, for parents with reservations to drop their children off. As an incentive to parents, you can charge slightly less for each child than you would for staying with just one kid. But, in the end, you will be making more per hour because more parents pay you for the same time. That is how you multiply your earning power.

Group babysitting services are needed any place adults gather. Ask the owners or managers of health and exercise spas, hair salons, or athletic clubs if they could use your babysitting service. When you hear about an adult party, ask the hostess if you can watch the children of her guests. Other places your services are welcome are churches, synagogues, volunteer organizations, or political campaign offices. Meetings held by women's clubs or religious groups are often announced in the newspaper. Call and ask if they need a sitter. When they hire you, get to the meeting fifteen minutes early to meet and greet the kids. Plan several games and stories. When the meeting ends, clean the room and have the children ready to go.

Be creative with your babysitting business. Call it a "private play school," and advertise to neighbors that you will give special classes for kids in exercise, painting, cooking, music, dance, or handicrafts. For legal reasons, make it clear that yours is not an accredited school and you are not a licensed teacher.

If you like the movies and theater, you can start an escort service where you take kids to movies, stage plays, puppet shows, or concerts. Figure out your expenses, including the price of your own ticket and refreshments for the kids, and add them to the price of your babysitting time to determine how much to charge for your service. Never take more children than you can watch.

One of the reasons babysitters make a lot is because it is often hard to find good ones, so parents are willing to pay well. You can offer a babysitter "finder" service. As a kid yourself, it is probably easier for you to find other kids to babysit. As a service to both the sitters and the parents, you help them find each other. Each pays you a small fee to make the match.

Other jobs to do if you like working with younger children is taking babies for stroller or baby-carriage rides, or walking older children to and from school or to the library. To do this, you need to be dependable and aware of basic safety rules. You can escort several children to school, but if you do, make sure you can manage the group easily and safely. You can charge by the hour, or a flat rate for the day or the whole week.

WOULD YOU RATHER BE AROUND OLDER PEOPLE?

Why not become a senior citizen's assistant? Older people often have trouble doing chores around the house. Most cannot afford to pay adult **wages** *for simply taking out the garbage, sweeping the driveway, or grocery shopping, but they would be happy to pay for your service. In addition to an hourly wage, you will be paid generously in wonderful stories of the good-old-days.*

If you like working with older people, you can read newspapers, magazines, books and mail aloud to them, write letters and cards, or make their telephone calls. You can also help with house-cleaning, garden work, and household repairs. If you are handy in the kitchen, you can prepare meals and clean up. And you can take them for a walk. To find people who need your help, contact retirement homes or community centers.

ARE YOU AN ANIMAL LOVER?

Most kids are. And there are plenty of services people will pay you to perform for pets. For example, pet owners like their beloved animals to smell fresh and clean and be well behaved. You can offer a pet grooming-and-training service where you shampoo the animals, give them flea and tick baths, brush their coats, and, perhaps, teach them tricks.

Also consider a pet-sitting service for your customers on vacation. If you have the space, you can build a kennel to keep the animals overnight or longer. But usually you can keep larger pets, like dogs and cats, in their own homes and just drop by to walk, feed, and water them each day their owner is away. For smaller pets, like hamsters, lizards, and fish, it may be easier to put them up in your room—in their own cages and tanks, of course! Make sure you know exactly what your customer expects you to do, that you can get along with the pet, and have enough food for the animals. Advertise your service at pet stores and veterinarians' offices.

If you really enjoy animals, try breeding them and selling their offspring for money. You can raise and sell hamsters, rabbits, gerbils, and, of course, dogs and cats. For people who have too

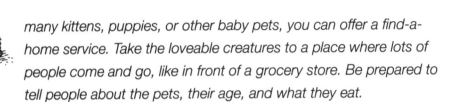

many kittens, puppies, or other baby pets, you can offer a find-a-home service. Take the loveable creatures to a place where lots of people come and go, like in front of a grocery store. Be prepared to tell people about the pets, their age, and what they eat.

ARE YOU THE ARTISTIC OR CREATIVE TYPE? *Then use your imagination to market your special talent. If you like to perform as a musician, magician, or juggler, and you are good, sell your services to stores, hotels, or restaurants that are known for entertainment. You can put on your own variety show, play, or puppet show, and charge admission.*

And what if your talent is knowing how to have a good time? Well, show other people how you do it by planning parties. Offer a complete service by selecting the theme of the party, setting tables, and cleaning up. You can do the entire party yourself or simply assist the parent. Sell yourself as a disc jockey at the party—especially if you have a great collection of tapes or CDs. Or, if you have a video camera, offer to tape the whole affair.

If you have a decent camera and are good at taking pictures, set up a photography business. People love pictures of their children and pets. Take fliers door-to-door offering to take photos of kids in their homes. You can also take pictures at music recitals, pet shows, family reunions, school dances, and weddings.

Anyone with a flair for wrapping presents could have a booming business at holiday times. Many organizations have Christmas fairs and bazaars where you can set up a booth. Stores without wrapping departments may let you set up a gift-wrapping table. Or you can offer to bring supplies to people's homes and wrap presents there. If you know calligraphy or have good handwriting, you can address envelopes for holiday greeting cards or party invitations.

CAN YOU TEACH ME THAT? *If you have a special skill, people will be interested in learning it, and they will pay you to teach them. Can you play a musical instrument? Speak another language?*

Repair a bicycle or fix a car? Program a computer? Twirl a baton? Type? Dance? Cook? Swim? Adults as well as children need lessons in these areas—and many more.

Students who get straight <u>A</u>s in a particular subject can easily tutor. But it requires patience. Remember, a subject easy for you is not easy for everyone. When you take a student, agree on what time to meet each week, perhaps twice a week for one hour. Charge by the hour. To drum up business, advertise at schools. Talk to your teachers and ask them to recommend you to students who need help and will pay for your service.

YOU'D RATHER SELL A PRODUCT THAN A SERVICE?

You can make money by selling any number of things: things you own, things you collect, things you make or bake, or even things you grow. Here are a few ideas. Can you think of other products to sell?

Things you own, do not want or like anymore, but could sell include toys, games, or sports equipment; old records, tapes, or CDs; old magazines, books, or comics; and, of course, clothes that you have outgrown.

Some items you can collect and sell are seashells, starfish, and sand dollars; or rocks, pine cones, mistletoe, and dried weeds. If you live near lakes or rivers, you can make money by selling worms and crickets for fish bait. You can also collect aluminum cans or glass bottles, to return to the store for a refund in many areas.

With a little imagination, you can sell things you make, like tie-dyed, silk-screened, or hand-painted T-shirts; candles made from blocks of wax and old crayons; or painted rock paperweights. If you are a computer whiz, create and sell computer-generated greeting cards and customized calendars, or fliers, banners, and yard signs for special occasions. Grown-ups go ga-ga over children's artwork, such as drawings, paintings, and handicrafts, so if you are the least bit talented, you can sell your creations at a backyard "art exhibit."

People are always hungry and thirsty, so if you set up a refreshment stand where people gather, you are bound to make money. You can buy pre-packaged snacks and soft drinks that you sell for a profit, or make your own goodies. Homemade cakes, cookies, candies, and sandwiches are big sellers. Parade routes, sports events, flea markets, community picnics, and club meetings are good places for the food-and-drink business.

If you have a "green thumb," you can turn gardening into money. Fresh herbs are popular. You can grow herbs in your house, year-round, and offer to package and sell them at the local grocery store or farmer's market. You can also grow and sell small houseplants. In the summer and fall, you can run a vegetable stand or sell bouquets of fresh-cut flowers.

As you can probably tell by now, there are hundreds of ways to make money. So, have you decided what you would like to do? Then, keep reading and get ready to start making money.

CHAPTER 4

Going Into Business

BIZ KIDS

NAME: Brandon   **AGE:** 10   **HOMETOWN:** Miami

EDUCATION: Currently in the fifth grade

WORK EXPERIENCE: I own and run a flower delivery service. I buy flowers from a wholesaler, arrange them in bouquets, and deliver them once a week to my customers. My cost is about $10 per arrangement and I charge $20. Before I started my business, which I call Bloomin' Express, I wrote a business plan to see if I was likely to get customers and make a profit. I also had to register my business with the state and get a peddler's license from the county. I use fliers to advertise my business and I also get customers through word-of-mouth. Right now I have eight customers and sales are up to $150 a month. My goal is to get 15 customers.

MONEY GOAL: Most of my profits go into savings for college. I also give 10 percent to my church.

CHAPTER 4
Going Into Business

Now that you know something about the language of business and you have identified a promising service or product, it is time to do some planning. For example, you need to figure out how much time you can work on your business, where you will buy your supplies and how much they will cost, how much you can charge your customers, and how much profit to expect. In this chapter, you will learn how to make a budget and set up a bookkeeping system to keep track of your hard-earned money.

THE BUSINESS PLAN Why bother planning? Well, although there is no magic formula for success, one rule holds true: *A business owner who fails to plan, plans to fail.* Just consider the statistics: of the one million new businesses that adults start each year, only 200,000 last more than six years. Successful entrepreneurs usually write up a clear statement of what they intend to accomplish—a **business plan**. Think of it as a map designed to keep you headed in the right direction—toward your business goal. There are six steps to follow when writing your business plan.

1. List Your Goals. First, figure out <u>where you want to go</u>— a set of goals to guide and inspire you. Think of a goal as a dream with a timetable. Be specific. Simply saying, "I want to be the best babysitter in town," is too vague. Saying, "I want to babysit ten hours a week and save enough money to buy a car in four years," is more precise and better. The key is to make your goals reasonable and measureable so that you can tell how close you are to reaching them. So, <u>Step Number One</u>: Make a list of your business goals. It can be as simple as: "I want to make $_____ by (*fill in the date*)" or as complicated as "I want to get _____ new customers every week, earn _____ percent profit by the first year, and grow big enough to hire _____ employees by (*fill in the date*)."

2. Name Your Business. Before you actually start your business, give it a name and come up with a **business concept**. That is, stop to think about exactly <u>what your business will be</u> and how it will be better or different from anyone else's. You have to check out your competition to see where you can make improvements. For example, can you **guarantee** that yours will be the lowest price around? Or promise **customer satisfaction** with a money-back guarantee if the customer isn't happy? Or, perhaps you can offer a more complete line. Rather than just mowing lawns, for instance, offer a more complete yard-care service with everything from watering and cutting to leaf raking. When you have a concept for your business, give it a name. Be creative. Names like "Betsy Brown's Bountiful Brownies" or "Larry's Do-It-All Lawn Care" are good and descriptive. <u>Step Number Two</u>: Give your business a name and, in a sentence or two, state what service or product you will be selling and how you will set yourself apart from the crowd.

3. Plan a Timetable. <u>How long you plan to be in business and how much time you can work each week</u> are important. What is your time frame? Do you want to work just through the summer for the next two or three years? Do you want to work during the school year, too? Will you stay in business through your high school senior year? Or do you want to turn it into a full-time occupation after you graduate? Remember, business requires at least a month of planning and organization before you can start making money. So, if you want to wash cars for a summer, you need to start planning in April and May. At that time, set up a work **schedule**, too. To run your business on a regular basis, you need to set aside at least ten hours per week. Do you have the time? Be realistic plotting your free hours. Remember to make time for eating, sleeping, school work, social activities, and, of course, play and relaxation. If you are in school, your maximum work time should not exceed twenty hours during a school week. Also, make sure your business hours are when your customers need you. If your only free time is between 6 A.M. and 8 A.M., a lemonade stand will not make much sense, will it? <u>Step Number Three</u>: Establish a timetable for your business and set up a weekly work schedule.

4. List the Costs. *To make money, you often have to spend money. So, part of planning means <u>figuring out how much money you need</u> not only to get started but to keep running your business. There are two types of business costs: variable and fixed. As the name suggests, **variable costs** vary—depending upon how much you spend on each customer or product. In other words, the more customers you have, the higher your variable costs. After all, the more cookies or muffins you sell, the more you have to spend on ingredients. For a car-wash service, you have variable costs for things like car shampoo, wax, and rags. To estimate what it costs to perform a service or make a product, you have to try it out a couple of times. For a cookie company, for example, you have to bake a sample batch of cookies. How much sugar, flour, butter, and other ingredients did you use? How much did the whole batch cost? Then, figure out what each cookie cost.*

* **Fixed costs** are expenses that do not change—no matter how many customers you have. Examples of fixed costs are office equipment, such as a desk or computer, a telephone and answering machine, or, perhaps, a lawn mower. In addition to those, you may have smaller start-up fixed costs, such as business cards, stationery, invoices, fliers, a yard sign, and, possibly, a uniform or special clothing. On top of that, there may be ongoing fixed costs— costs that occur every month—such as advertising expenses, telephone bills, and office supplies. <u>Step Number Four</u>: Make a list of all your variable and fixed costs.*

5. Establish a Price. *Now that you know what it costs to be a biz kid, figure out <u>how much you have to charge your customers</u> to make it worth your while. Keep in mind, your price must be high enough to cover costs and earn you decent money, but low enough to attract customers. One method for setting a price is to base it on the competition. Call your competitors and ask what they charge and what they offer for the price. If you set your price equal to or higher than the competition, you should offer something special— better quality, quicker service, or a feature no one else offers.*

Another method for setting a price is to base it on how much you want to earn for the time you put in. Say you want to earn $5 per hour. How long does it take to make your product or perform your service? Verify your time estimate by practicing a few times. Also consider your variable costs. Before you start up a car-washing business, ask your parents if you may try your skill on their car. If it takes you two hours to do a thorough job and your material costs are $2 for a capful of car shampoo, a quarter jar of car wax, and some rags, you have to charge $12 to make your targeted $5 per hour. ($5 x 2 hours + $2 in variable costs = $12.) If your competition charges only $10, you are taking too long to perform the job or your wage expectations are too high. You either have to accept a lower hourly wage, work faster, or pick another business venture. Step Number Five: Establish your price based on your time and costs and what your competition charges.

6. Calculate Your Profit. *The final step of your business plan puts it all together to <u>show whether or not you can earn a profit</u>, based on your estimates of costs, prices, and how many customers you will have. The most difficult part of this last step is figuring out how many customers you can expect. The best advice is not to overestimate sales, especially in the first few months. Unless you line up a lot of business before you begin, it takes some time for news about your business to get around and for your reputation to grow. A way to get a handle on your prospects is to find out how much business your competition gets. Also, ask potential customers, such as friends, family, and neighbors, whether they might buy your product or service. Keep in mind that some businesses, like snow shoveling services, are seasonal, that is, they are only busy at certain times of the year. Step Number Six: Calculate how much profit your business can expect. Multiply the price you plan to charge times the number of products you plan to sell or customers you hope to serve and subtract your costs. Is there anything left over? If so, congratulations! It looks like your business could be a success.*

But what if it looks like your costs are greater than your sales? In that case, instead of a profit, you will have a loss. Thank goodness you discovered this in the planning stage! As you can see, planning before you start can save money and headaches later. If it looks like your business will not produce much money, you should think about raising prices, cutting costs, or picking a different business. Or, to make it work, maybe you simply have to find more time. To achieve success, you undoubtedly have to make a few sacrifices. Are you willing to give up a favorite activity, like watching TV? If not, maybe you are not ready to be a biz kid.

BUDGETING AND BOOKKEEPING   One key to success: in the start-up phase, do not spend money on anything that doesn't produce money. For instance, a new desk will definitely not bring extra cash, but a new advertising flier might. So, where should you put your money? In the flier, of course!

A second key to success: keep track of every penny. For this task, you first need to develop a monthly budget. A budget is simply a written list of all your income (how much money you expect to receive) and all your expenses (how much money you think you will spend). Begin by putting down how much you are starting with and where it came from (allowances, gifts, loans, money earned from doing jobs or selling things). Once you know the amount of money you can spend, you can make sure you do not spend more than you actually have. If it looks like your expenses will exceed your income, that is a problem. You will either have to earn more or spend less.

By the way, if you make $400 or more from your business, you are required by federal law to pay taxes. In that case, you have to keep records to back up your tax return information. You can keep all your records on little scraps of paper stuffed in a shoebox. That meets government standards, but makes it difficult to see whether you are making a profit or owe taxes.

Before you know whether you are making or losing money, you have to set up a system to keep track of what is being spent and what is being earned. Business people keep track of income

*and expenses by preparing an **Income Statement**—sometimes called a **Profit and Loss Statement**—at least once a month. This accounting system starts with a bookkeeping record, which you need to update every week. Make photocopies of the blank form on page 86 or buy an accounting book from an office supply store.*

*To simplify your bookkeeping, insist on payment from your customers at the time you do the work or sell your product. Keep track of this income with a two-part **invoice**. One copy goes to the customer and you keep the other one. Then, when you enter the income in your bookkeeping record, list the invoice number. (You can buy invoice forms from an office supply store or make copies of the one on page 87.)*

Just as you keep track of your income, keep all your expense receipts and file them every week. If possible, pay for all your expenses by check. That provides a backup record. Many banks do not let kids have checking accounts of their own. See if you can get your parents to co-sign for you, or find a bank that welcomes kids.

At the end of every month, find out whether you have made any money by preparing a Profit and Loss (P&L) Statement. Make copies of the blank P&L statement on page 86 for each month of the year. From your weekly bookkeeping records, add up all your income. Then add up all your expenses. Subtract the expenses from your income. If you have more income than expenses (and, therefore, the number is positive), you have a profit. If not, you have a loss.

If you have a loss, do not get discouraged. One bad month is not a disaster. Of course, you cannot afford to have too many profitless months, but do not give up before you analyze why you are not making money. Maybe terrible weather kept your customers away. Or your expenses were unusually high this month because you took advantage of a store's sale to build an inventory of raw materials, like flour and sugar if you are a cake baker. That means next month's expenses will be much lower and will probably make up for your losses. But that will happen only if you keep at it.

CHAPTER 5

Money Basics

BIZ KIDS

NAME: Nicole   **AGE:** 12   **HOMETOWN:** Glendale

EDUCATION: I'm in the seventh grade

WORK EXPERIENCE: I have a pet-sitting and pet-grooming business. When my customers go on vacation, I will feed their birds, cats, dogs, fish—or whatever—every day and make sure they have enough water. My rates are pretty reasonable. I charge just $5 a day. To wash and groom a dog, I charge $7 to $8, depending on how big the dog is. That's half the price a professional service would charge. I put the money I earn in a savings account I opened at a nearby bank.

PERSONAL: My favorite subjects in school are language arts, reading, and spelling. I collect stickers as a hobby. And I love animals; my family owns two dogs, four birds, and five fish.

MONEY GOAL: To save enough money to buy a car when I'm 16.

CHAPTER 5
Money Basics

So far, all we have talked about is how to make money. We haven't talked about money itself or what happens to it after you earn it. A smart biz kid knows not only how to make money but how to spend it wisely, how to borrow it when necessary, how to save or invest it, and, perhaps most important, when to be generous with it.

You may have heard people say, "Money is the root of all evil." Well, money is neither incredibly wonderful nor terribly evil. Basically, it is a device that makes it easier to trade one thing for another. You trade your hard work for metal coins and paper bills that allow you to buy things you need and want. And, of course, much good can be done with money when people use it to help those less fortunate. You will feel better about yourself and enjoy your money more if you share some. You might use it to buy a gift for someone or give money to an organization that helps the needy.

TRACKING YOUR MONEY Before you start spending your money—on yourself or anyone else—set up a method of tracking where your money comes from and where it goes. This is especially important when you run a business. Keeping track of how much you have, what you are spending it on, and knowing whether you can afford to buy what you want are the secrets to money success. As you learned in the last chapter, a budget helps.

For a clear picture of what you are spending your money on, keep a written record of all your spending for a month. Studying your spending habits shows where you can cut down and save. Then you can set up a budget. First, list all the money you have from gifts, allowance, running your business or other jobs. Then, list what you have bought or spent your money on during the month. How much money do you have left? Then, before you buy anything else, ask: What do I want to buy? How much does it cost? How much have I saved so far? How much more do I need? At that point, you can see how much longer it will take you to save enough for your purchase. Or, you may decide not to wait that long and you borrow money to pay for it.

BORROWING MONEY   Borrowing money can be painful. It is not easy to find someone willing to lend money to a kid just getting started in business. And, of course, you will have to pay the money back— usually with interest. That means for every dollar you borrow, you may have to return $1.10 (or more) to the lender. Ouch! That hurts.

So, before you buy a brand new lawn mower or expensive computer to get your business going, think about ways to keep your costs low to save money. Take advantage of every free resource you can get your hands on. For example, adults are usually happy to lend equipment or supplies to young entrepreneurs. Maybe you borrow a copy machine, a typewriter, or whatever else you need, instead of buying your own fancy equipment. Or rent it in the beginning to keep expenses down, and, then, buy it later out of future **earnings**. Get by on a shoestring, especially in the beginning. If you must buy right away, check out a local thrift shop or Goodwill store and scan the classified ads in the local newspaper for used equipment and supplies.

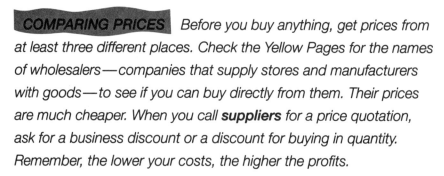

COMPARING PRICES   Before you buy anything, get prices from at least three different places. Check the Yellow Pages for the names of wholesalers—companies that supply stores and manufacturers with goods—to see if you can buy directly from them. Their prices are much cheaper. When you call **suppliers** for a price quotation, ask for a business discount or a discount for buying in quantity. Remember, the lower your costs, the higher the profits.

BANK ACCOUNTS   Do not forget to keep accurate records of the money you spend (your expenses) and the money you take in (your income). In addition to the bookkeeping record mentioned in the last chapter, consider opening a bank account. The best account is a **checking account**, which lets you keep money in a safe place and use it anytime you need it.

When you open a checking account, you get **checks** from your <u>bank</u> and a <u>register</u> for keeping track of the money you put in and take out of your account. Each time you put money into your bank account, you fill out a <u>deposit slip</u> and record the amount of

deposit in your register. To get money out of the bank to pay for something, you write a check to the person or store you want to give the money to. Write down the information (to whom you wrote the check and for how much) in your register and subtract it from the total for the remaining balance. Keeping track of what you have deposited and spent tells you how much money you have in the bank.

Checks are easier and safer than cash. Instead of carrying wads of dollars to pay for what you buy, you can write a check. You can also mail checks to pay bills. And a check that has cleared the bank and been returned to you is proof you paid a bill. So, besides your bookkeeping system, you have backup records of expenses and income. You might need this to calculate your taxes and to prove to the **Internal Revenue Service (IRS)** that you are a serious business operator.

You may have to shop around for a bank that caters to kids. Some banks do not open checking accounts for anyone under eighteen. If you are under eighteen and cannot find a bank in your area willing to open an account for you, see if you can get a joint checking account with your parents. Otherwise, open a **passbook savings account**. A bank will open a savings account for anyone with a Social Security number, and every American must have a Social Security number—sometimes called a **taxpayer identification number**—by the age of one.

A savings account can be a great little money-maker. As long as the money stays in your account, the bank pays you **interest**. It differs from a checking account, because to take out money, you must go to the bank to make a **withdrawal**. But it helps track the money you spend on your business and the money you earn—measures of your growth and success.

Keep in mind that someday you may want to sell your business, and potential buyers will want to look at your money records. The more accurate, the better, and a bank account is most reliable. Whether you open a checking account or a savings account, a bank account is a good way to learn banking. If you ever want to borrow money from the bank, it may help you qualify for a loan.

PRINCIPAL

INTEREST

LOANS   A **loan** is an amount of money that a person borrows for a certain period of time. In addition to paying the actual loan amount—known as **principal**—a borrower has to pay a fee for the use of the money. This is called interest and is calculated as a percent of the loan amount. For example, if you borrow $200 for one year at 10 percent interest, you would owe $200 (the principal) plus $20 (the interest, which is $200 times 10 percent) or $220 at the end of the year. In most cases, you pay off a loan in stages by, say, making one payment each month. Your monthly payment for this one-year loan would be $220 divided by 12 months or $18.33.

You might be able to reduce your monthly payments by stretching the loan for a longer period, but the longer you take to repay the money, the more interest you have to pay. In this example, if you wanted to pay back the $200 over a two-year period instead of one year, you would owe $40 in interest ($200 times 10 percent times 2 years). Your monthly payments would be just $10 ($240 divided by 24 months), but you would be pay back a total of $240 for that $200 loan. As you can see, interest really adds up. Unfortunately, that is the cost of **credit**.

TAKE SOME CREDIT   By the way, credit is not a right. It is a privilege. People who want to borrow money must prove they are responsible and they can afford to make their monthly principal and interest payments. A bank will give credit only to someone it feels sure will pay back the loan. That is why children often have trouble getting bank loans. They do not have a history to prove they are creditworthy.

The best place to start looking for a bank loan is the bank in which you have a savings or checking account. The bank's **lending officer** will ask you all kinds of questions about yourself, your education, where you live, other debts you owe, what you plan to do with the money, and how you expect to repay the loan. So, before you ask for a loan, prepare a brief **resumé** of your experience and a business plan that spells out your intentions. If you are enthusiastic and your plan shows you will definitely earn enough money to pay it *back, the bank just might lend you the amount you need.*

*There are also things you should ask your banker. Of course you will want to know what interest rate is being charged and how much you will have to pay each month. But also find out whether there are charges if your payment is late. Some banks actually charge people for repaying a loan early, so ask whether there is a prepayment penalty, too. First-time borrowers often must put up something valuable, such as a car, stocks, or bonds, as **collateral**. Ask at what point the bank can take your collateral away from you if you fail to make a loan payment (**default**). Chances are, if you do not have something the bank considers valuable enough for collateral, a friend or relative will have to <u>co-sign</u>, that is, promise to repay the loan if you can't.*

RAISING MONEY *If you are turned down by a bank, do not get upset—get smart. You are not the first kid to get a rejection from a bank, nor will you be the last. There are other ways to get quick cash. Look around your room for things you do not use but someone else would buy. Are there old videos, books, or computer games you could give up? Ask family or friends to donate things to a **garage sale** to raise cash for your business. Are there chores you can do for them? After rummaging around, are you still short on cash? Then maybe you should pick a venture that does not need a large initial investment.*

As a last resort, talk to your parents or another adult you are close to about a loan. If they can afford it and your business plan shows you will be able to pay them back within a reasonable time, they may be willing to give you the chance that a big bank would not. But be as business-like and responsible with this loan as you would with a bank loan. Telling your Mom or Dad that you are willing to pay back a loan <u>with interest</u> lets them know you are money wise and you recognize the fact that money is never free.

Begin by perfecting your business plan as described in Chapter Four. In your list of variable and fixed costs, include your monthly loan payment as a fixed cost (you have to repay the loan no matter how many customers you have). Make sure you can still make a profit (subtract your expected costs from your expected income). Then, write up a brief **IOU**—known as a **loan document**. State the loan terms: principal amount of the loan (what you will get), interest rate (in percent), cost of interest (principal multiplied by interest rate), total amount to be repaid (principal plus cost of interest), length of the loan (how long you have to pay it back), payment plan (how much you will pay every week or month), and date of final payment. (See page 88 for a sample loan document.) Both you and your lender should sign and date the loan document. Then, stick to it!

SAVING   You are way ahead of the game if you never have to borrow. How do you stay out of debt? By saving. Saving money is putting it away for later use—for your business and personal reasons. Saving enough money to buy a car outright or pay for a major trip means no loan payments. And saving now for college, which can cost thousands of dollars, will make it easier to afford the school of your choice. Experts say to save at least ten percent of the money you earn.

There are two basic ways to save your money: in a piggy bank or other container in your house or in a bank savings account. As you have already learned, a bank will pay you to keep your money in it, and the longer your money is in a savings account, the more interest you earn. On top of that, money in a bank is less likely to be lost or stolen.

Being a responsible biz kid means a lot more than just keeping track of money, but starting and maintaining a set of records establishes the habit of being careful about money. Remember, when you borrow, you have to pay it all back plus a little extra (that dreaded interest). But interest works for you when you save money in a place that pays you to keep it there. Managing money can be simple once you understand you cannot spend more than you have and that your financial future depends on how well you budget and plan today.

CHAPTER 6

Marketing Your Business

BIZ KIDS

NAME: Jon   **AGE:** 17   **HOMETOWN:** League City
EDUCATION: High school senior
WORK EXPERIENCE: Seven years ago, I started out repairing dirtbikes, motorbikes, and go-carts as a hobby. For the past five years, I've operated my own small engine repair shop. My primary business is lawn mower repair. I advertise my business with business cards and a magnetic sign on the side of the family truck, but I get most of my business by word-of-mouth. The going labor rate for small engine repair is $35 an hour and I only charge $25 an hour, so people tell their friends. A few times last summer I had days when I did $1000 in business by selling a riding mower I'd fixed or repairing a tractor mower. I get a lot of business because I am the only repair person in my area to offer pickup and delivery service.

CHAPTER 6
Marketing Your Business

Managing money is an important life skill, but even more crucial to running a business is finding customers and keeping them happy. After all, if you do not have customers, you will not have money to manage. In this chapter, you will learn how to get customers by doing serious marketing.

Marketing is getting information about you and your product or service out to prospective customers and finding a suitable price for your work. No doubt you have seen the way toy manufacturers and cereal makers use magazine ads and television commercials to advertise their goods. Similarly, you have to advertise your kid biz, but you should use cheaper forms of **advertising**. One free way to promote yourself is by publicity and **public relations**. And, finally, you have to set a price for your product or service that is high enough to make money, but low enough to attract customers.

SELLING YOURSELF As any successful salesperson will tell you, despite the best product or service in the world, if your customers do not have confidence in you, nothing will make them buy. So, the first thing you must do is <u>sell yourself</u>. That means convincing your customers they can trust you to do the best job possible.

Talk about your business to everyone you know, and when you do, give thought to the impression you make. A neat appearance counts, especially with grown-ups. So, dress for success. That is, look clean and tidy, and wear nice clothes—not grubby, torn jeans (even though they may be your personal favorites). You might even wear a uniform, such as a T-shirt, jacket, or cap, with your business name on it. Have clean nails, teeth, and hair, too. Use good manners, and be generous with words like "please" and "thank you." Being polite, friendly, and courteous, with a nice, big smile shows customers you can be trusted to do a good job.

USING "POWER WORDS" When discussing your kid biz with potential clients, use **power words** to describe your product or service. These words set off a positive emotional response because *they explain how the customer's life will be easier, less costly, or more pleasant. Words such as "trouble-free," "money-saving," "dependable," "reliable," or "guaranteed" are all good power words. When you tell, you sell.*

*Of course, once you make a promise, you have to keep it. If you say you are dependable or reliable, you better show up on time or have someone trained and ready to substitute for you if you cannot be there. When you finish your job, thank your customers for their business. Make sure your customers are satisfied with your service, and ask for suggestions for improvement. Your best business **prospects** are happy customers. They will spread the word to their friends and neighbors and you will get even more money-making work.*

GETTING RECOMMENDED   *Think about others who might recommend you. Most kids start out working for their parents. Since it helps to be recommended by adults, your parents can help by telling people you want jobs. You will be amazed at how fast this kind of information travels. Some organizations provide free referral services that you should check out. Ask at your local YMCA, Better Business Bureau, real estate agency, or even your school to see if they have a community referral service. If your kid biz improves business for local shop owners, they may refer potential customers to you. For example, if you offer a delivery or buying service, they would be delighted to recommend you.*

TARGETING CUSTOMERS   *Think about who your customers might be and where they are most likely to hear about you. This is called **targeting** your customers—or figuring out where people who need your services might be found. For instance, if you want to babysit, visit places where you find parents with young children, such as a park or playground. Brandee asked the parents at her Kingman, Arizona, church if they could use her babysitting service. Since these people knew and trusted her, she got plenty of work. If you plan a lawn-care service business, walk around your* *neighborhood and look for yards that need mowing. John, who likes to do outdoor work, rang the doorbells of houses with dirty cars in the driveway or overgrown yards. People answering the door were immediately won over by his bright smile and he often got the job.*

DOOR-TO-DOOR SELLING *What John did to get customers in his Phoenix neighborhood is known as door-to-door selling and it can be used to peddle your services or a product. You will have a higher success rate if you go door-to-door when most people are at home, such as early evening (before dark) or on weekends. But people get annoyed when disturbed while eating, so avoid the dinner hour. Dress neatly and always use the sidewalk. Ring doorbells three times. If there is no answer, leave a note or a flier that describes your product or service. But when the door opens, greet your potential customer (your prospect) with a friendly smile and cheerful greeting. Also, be prepared with a snappy, enthusiastic sales pitch—a one minute description of who you are and what you are selling. Look your prospect straight in the eye and explain the benefits of your product or service. Be ready to provide a reference from a neighbor, friend, or teacher. You can say something like, "Mrs. Jones across the street can tell you about the great job I did on her backyard." Even if prospects turn you down—this time— leave business cards or fliers behind so they can contact you if they change their minds. Or they may pass your phone number to a friend who could use your service.*

TELEPHONE SELLING *Although not as effective as person-to-person selling, selling over the phone is another way to market a product or service. But you have to talk fast. If you do not identify yourself and get your message across in the first ten to fifteen seconds, your prospects lose patience. So, get their attention by being enthusiastic. Smiling while talking is reflected in your voice and endears you to the person on the other end of the line. Have a positive attitude. Rather than saying, "I don't suppose you need me to wash your car, do you?" a **closing technique** that works is "When do you want me to start?" or "How many do you want?"*

At all times be smart about how you sell and to whom you sell. Did a new family just move in on your block? Be a good neighbor by offering a free hour of unpacking, babysitting, or errand running—your own personal welcome wagon gift. Once they see what a good worker you are, you may have a steady, paying customer. Another inventive way of getting customers is to sell yourself as a present. For example, the friends or relatives of a new mother or a bedridden patient might hire you to do her house cleaning or dishwashing or yard work. What a truly useful gift that is! Of course, you should point that out in your sales pitch.

WORD-OF-MOUTH POWER Never underestimate the power of "word-of-mouth." It is the most powerful and lasting of all advertising. After all, every person you work for or to whom you sell a product probably knows at least fifty people through work or social contacts—fifty people who could become your customers. Any way you can get people talking positively about your business, such as your dependability and quality of work, is good for your reputation. But, remember, even one unhappy customer can damage your business, and if you do a lousy job, the power of word-of-mouth advertising can work against you. The key to success, then, is to keep your customers happy.

ADVERTISING Friends, neighbors, and relatives are all good prospects when you start selling your services or products. But to make your business grow, eventually you have to go beyond this circle of acquaintances to find new customers. To advertise your kid biz to many different people, put up posters, signs, and fliers or pass out business cards with your name and phone number so that customers call you instead of you calling them.

Before you begin to advertise, discuss this idea with your parents. They may feel that putting your name and phone number in a public place is not safe or may attract undesirable phone calls. So, they may tell you it's okay to advertise yourself at your church or synagogue or in your own apartment building, but it is not okay to *put your fliers up at the supermarket or local bar. Don't list your age or your last name. Think about using a company name or nickname so you can tell when a person is calling you about business. Talk with your parents about working for strangers before accepting any job. Let your parents check out your plans so they know you are following good safety practices.*

Posters and signs work best for advertising things such as garage sales, lemonade stands, car-washing services, and yard work. If people passing by can see you working, put out a large sign saying who you are, what you are doing, and how to reach you. For example, if you are washing windows, you might display a sign that says "WALLY AT WORK. For complete window-washing service, call WALLY 555-5555." Make signs out of poster board, butcher paper, shelf paper, or even old sheets. Use bold colors and make the letters big enough to read from across the street. Get permission from customers to put up the sign on their property while you work. Also, carry a stack of business cards or index cards with your name and number that you can hand out to people who stop to ask you about your service.

You can be a moving billboard by wearing a T-shirt or jacket with your biz name on it or by putting signs or bumper stickers on your vehicle. Whether you use a wagon or get around on a bike, skateboard, or moped, or in a car or truck, your sign is a potential draw to everyone you pass. Jon Drew of League City, Texas, who has run his own small engine repair shop since he was twelve, put a magnetic sign on the side of the family truck to advertise his business. People who see him picking up or dropping off a lawn-mower or motorbike he has fixed and need that type of service can get his name and phone number off the sign.

FLIERS *Fliers are an excellent advertising tool more flexible than signs. You can pass them out, mail them, post them on a bulletin board, or put them under car windshield wipers. Fliers also give you more room than signs to describe your product or service. In addition to your business name and phone number, include what*

makes you qualified to do the job, such as experience, awards, and good references. Or explain what makes your product unique or special and why you are better than the competition. Do you offer lower prices? Faster delivery? Guaranteed results?

It costs just a few cents apiece to photocopy a homemade flier. You can dress it up with eye-catching artwork or stickers and a neatly drawn border. Come up with a catchy phrase or **slogan** so people will remember it. Look at ads in magazines and newspapers and listen to TV commercials for words the advertising experts use to entice you to buy. Words like "fabulous," "supreme," and "wonderful," might work, but customers are more likely to jump when they see words such as "reliable" and "dependable."

Fliers are a good way to get the word out, but be cautious choosing where to distribute them. It is illegal to put fliers in mailboxes, so they must be hand delivered to your prospects' doors. In addition to passing them out in your neighborhood, give them to shopkeepers and managers of local businesses, but okay it with your parents first. And, before tacking them up on bulletin boards, ask permission.

BUSINESS CARDS You can post these small, 2-inch by 3½-inch cards with your name and phone number just about everywhere—on bulletin boards at grocery stores, laundromats, restaurants, coffee shops, libraries, health clubs, record shops, schools, or community centers. But before you do, ask about special posting rules, and have permission from your parents, too.

Business cards are even cheaper than fliers. The typical price for 500 ordinary black-and-white cards with your name and number is about $10 to $15. But for a fraction of that cost, buy some plain index cards and make your own. In big letters, write your name and phone number and a short description of the work you do, such as babysitting or pet care, along with the available times and the price. Having your cards ready to hand out means prospective clients don't have to jot down the information.

NEWSPAPER ADS *To get your message across to many, many potential customers, try advertising in a newspaper. Small town newspaper ads are affordable, but ad rates in large cities are extremely expensive. The ad rate depends on the circulation, that is, how many people actually receive the publication.*

Classified ads, or "want ads," are not fancy, but they are least expensive. These ads are lumped together, usually at the back of the paper, and you are charged by the word or line. A classified ad of twenty words typically costs from $5 to $20 for every day it runs. One reason for a want ad is that people looking in a specific classified section are usually interested in finding your particular service or product. In a sense, you have a targeted audience. Display ads are bigger than classified ads, and can use fancy typestyles or artwork, but they can be expensive. A small display ad, about the size of a business card, can cost more than $100 a day in some big-city papers.

The least expensive papers to advertise in are local shopping guides, sometimes called "Penny Savers" or "Dollar Savers." They are cheaper because their circulation is limited to your area. That is good because you get your message across to your neighborhood, not areas twenty miles away.

Another inexpensive—if not free—place to advertise is in a local newsletter. Organizations such as religious groups and clubs publish regular bulletins for their members. Your parents may know about alumni associations or groups such as Elks, Knights of Columbus, Lions clubs, Kiwanis clubs, or Toastmasters, that will publicize your product or service for little or no money.

By the way, no matter where you advertise, never promise anything you cannot fulfill. False advertising is unethical and against the law.

PUBLICITY *The flip side of advertising is publicity. Unlike advertising, which costs money, publicity is free. But, publicity gives you no control over what the media—the newspaper, magazines, radio, or TV—say about you. And, to get publicity, you usually have* to do something newsworthy to get the attention of the press. Often you can get publicity by issuing a press release or staging a media event or happening.

A **press release** is a statement that you write up describing your business and how you got started, along with anything unique or interesting about you or your product or service. If you can tie your business into an important community event or relate it to a famous person, your press release is more likely to receive attention. It should be typed, double-spaced, and no more than a page long. At the top, list a contact person (probably you) along with a phone number and address. Ask an adult to review your press release. Then send it to the local media, including newspapers and radio and TV stations.

You may be deemed newsworthy simply because you are young and ambitious. But, more likely, you will have to do something to get media coverage. After all, it's supposed to be news. You might plan an event with you and your business right on center stage. For example, to promote your lawn-care service, you can sponsor a "lawn-of-the-month" contest and award a small prize to the neighbor with the nicest looking yard. Before and after you award your prize, send out a press release announcing this special event along with the details of your unique kid biz.

Another way to drum up media attention is to involve your business in activities that benefit the community. For example, if you want to make money as a clown or entertainer, donate time by making public appearances at a children's hospital or retirement home. Or adopt a worthy cause. If you run a pet-care business, you can **donate** some of your profits to, say, the World Wildlife Fund. Then, make it public. Almost every successful entrepreneur has a well-developed sense of social responsibility and a desire to give something back to the world. Besides, the publicity your business receives from your good works is better than any advertising.

AVOIDING THE "PRICING TRAP"   But all the publicity and promotion in the world will not help you if your price is so high that customers will not buy. On the other hand, you can lose your shirt if you do not charge enough to cover costs. Biz kids say one of the hardest steps is figuring out what to charge. Part of the problem is a lot of kids are just too embarrassed to talk about money. But you have to get used to talking about money to be in business.

The best way to avoid the "pricing trap" is to do a little **market research**. Talk to potential customers—as well as your competitors—before you start your business. How much would the customer be willing to pay? And how does that compare to the **going rate** in your area? Ask your friends how much they earn for the same job. Your parents can ask their friends what they pay for similar jobs.

If you are just beginning, you may have to charge less than the competition. The younger or less experienced you are, the less you will make at first. When Brian found out that some of his friends charged $35 to mow an acre of lawn, he started out charging $30 an acre. And when new people moved into the neighborhood, he offered to do the first job free or for a $5 to $10 discount, depending on the lawn size. Now he gets more calls than the more experienced kids who charge more. So, Brian will probably raise his rates.

For jobs that are often done by adult professionals, such as yard maintenance, housework, and car-care, your parents may know the going rate. Since you are not a professional, it is best to charge somewhat less for your services, even if you feel you will do just as good a job. Jon makes a whopping $25 an hour repairing lawn mowers and other small engines, but since the going rate is $35 an hour at the local repair shop, Jon's customers see him as a bargain. Needless to say, Jon is always busy.

Everyone loves a **bargain**. From time to time, why not give your customers a deal? Give your most valued customers a ten percent-off coupon or throw in extra work and let them know you are not charging for it. Their gratitude will come back to you every time they recommend you to a friend—a potential customer for you.

Make your pricing consistent. You do not want a prospective client to hear about a special deal for the neighbor next door that is not available to him. If you make a special introductory offer to one first-time client, make it to them all.

Of course, the whole idea of being in business is to make a profit. The only way to do that is to charge enough to cover all your costs. Sit down with a calculator and figure out how much you would end up with after you pay for the supplies, equipment, advertising, etc., that you need to be in business. It should amount to something, but do not worry if it is not a lot. You can always raise your prices later if you are a big success. In the meantime, you have a good time learning how to run a business.

HARD WON SUCCESS   Unfortunately, success rarely comes easy. All good salespeople expect some amount of rejection. And, because you are young, you probably will get plenty. But do not take it personally. Some people will say "No" because they simply do not need your product or service. This is no reason to feel defeated. For your more stubborn prospects who do not want to hire you because you are too young or lack experience, you can offer to guarantee results. Tell them if they are not satisfied with your work, they can have their money back. Then be prepared to back up your promise with a job well done. But even if you must return their money, be polite and friendly and do your best to please. Tell them it will not happen again.

Building a clientele—or a set of customers—requires hard work, a lot of hustle, and doing a great job for clients. You have probably heard the saying, "The customer is always right." Well, the secret to keeping customers happy is to make that your motto. Treat even the rudest and most disrespectful person with courtesy. When talking with prospective customers, put yourself in their shoes. Listen to what they say they need, like, or want, and then give them exactly that. Your goal is to cultivate satisfied customers who will spread the word about what a terrific biz kid you are. A word-of-mouth recommendation from a satisfied customer is the cheapest and most reliable form of advertising there is.

CHAPTER 7

You, the Law, and Reporting Requirements

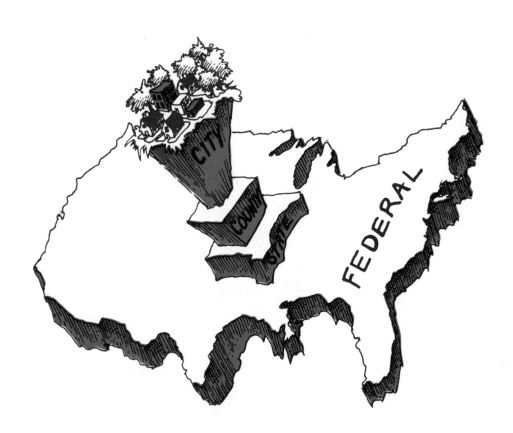

BIZ KIDS

NAME: Brandee **AGE:** 16 **HOMETOWN:** Dolan Springs

EDUCATION: Attending junior year of high school

WORK EXPERIENCE: Certified babysitter. I got my certificate in babysitting after taking a week-long course offered by the Fire Department. Besides the usual one-on-one babysitting, I provide "group" sitting at bargain rates: Just $2 per hour for the first child and $1 per hour for each additional child. Most of my customers hear about me from other satisfied customers. I have also worked as a cashier in my grandfather's grocery store and as a typesetter at the local Dollar Saver.

PERSONAL: I volunteer as a group leader for a church youth group. I'm a member of my high school Spanish and Journalism Clubs.

MONEY GOAL: To raise enough money for a class trip to Spain. To save for college.

CAREER GOAL: Teacher

CHAPTER 7
You, the Law, and Reporting Requirements

Your safety and well-being are important. That is why laws and regulations protect you when you work. Some laws apply specifically to kids to ensure they are not mistreated by employers. Other regulations, in the form of permits and licenses, are intended to protect consumers. And, finally, all business owners and money-earners must live by rules are intended to raise taxes, which help pay for everything from schools and roads to the United States military. As a biz kid, you may have to deal with all four levels of government: federal, state, county, and city or town.

In 1938, Congress passed the **Fair Labor Standards Act**. At first glance, these laws appear to discriminate against kids by prohibiting them from certain kinds of work or from working too many hours. Actually, these federal laws are to keep employers from hiring children, and they are primarily meant to protect children from abusive employers. So, for example, if you are under sixteen years old, you are not allowed to do jobs that the government considers "hazardous," including dangerous window-washing jobs that require standing on ladders or scaffolding or jobs in the mining or manufacturing industries.

Technically, anyone under the age of fourteen may be employed only by his or her parents in non-hazardous jobs. (The only exceptions are for child actors, newspaper delivery, or home wreath making.) But no child has ever been prosecuted for babysitting or mowing grass for the neighbors, and the law does not say specifically that kids may not be **self-employed**. According to federal law, however, anyone under fourteen is not supposed to work more than three hours on a school day, more than eighteen hours during a school week, or more than eight hours a day during vacations. If you want additional information on how the federal **child labor laws** affect you, contact your local Department of Labor office.

Some states have child labor laws stricter than the federal laws, and they vary from state to state. In New York, for example, if you plan to work after 10 P.M., you need written permission from both your parents and your school. That is to make sure you don't *fall behind in your schoolwork. Call your state Department of Labor or Office of Employment to see how your business is affected by state laws. The phone number is in the phone book under "Government Offices." When you call, say your age and the type of work you plan to do. And ask them to send you their* **pamphlet**.

SAFETY FIRST *These rules are meant to ensure your safety, so, by all means, obey them. Safety also means your parents know exactly where you are and how they can reach you at all times. When a responsible adult knows when you are to be home, you can be assured that someone will take action immediately if you are overdue or not heard from. Also, discuss with your parents how you will get to and from your work. Is it all right to take public transportation or to ride your bike? Or will it be too dark when the job is done, in which case will someone give you a ride?*

While on the job, protect yourself and others from physical harm. Can you care for minor injuries, such as cuts, bruises, or sprains? Have a first-aid kit available. Memorize the emergency phone numbers for the police and fire department. Take lessons in first-aid.

Before Brandee started as a babysitter, she took a class in safe childcare from the local fire department. She even learned how to give cardiopulmonary resuscitation (CPR) in case of a heart attack. When she completed the course, the fire prevention bureau awarded her a certificate as a "certified babysitter." Not only did it give Brandee confidence, but it got her jobs from parents who knew she would be a conscientious and responsible sitter.

For safety's sake, in your quest to earn lots of money, do not agree to do jobs bigger than you can do. For example, do not try to lift something too heavy or large for you. And riskier jobs, such as chimney cleaning, should be left for an experienced adult. Finally, never accept a ride from someone you do not know. If the job requires transportation, have someone you can trust drive you around. Never accept a ride from a stranger—no matter how nice he or she may seem.

Safety requires good judgment. Being a responsible biz kid means living within the government's rules and regulations. If you are in doubt, ask an adult.

SOCIAL SECURITY *Your parents probably have already helped you out with one of the biggest governmental agencies, the **Social Security Administration**. That is where you go for your Social Security card, which everyone must have by the age of one. Ask your parents to show you your Social Security card. See that nine-digit number? You are the only one in the world to have that number, and you keep it for life. It is like a worker identification number that lets the government keep track of you and your money.*

*The Social Security Administration is an agency of the United States Department of Health and Human Services. Think of it as a big savings account. Every time you pay **income taxes**, a certain part of your taxes goes to the Social Security Administration. Then, when you get to be sixty-two years old, the age at which many people retire from work, you get to withdraw it. How much you can take out each month depends on how much you made during your working life.*

It is against the law to work or earn money without a Social Security card. So, if for some reason you do not already have yours, get it now. It is free, and you can get it by mail. Call the Social Security Administration at 800-772-1213 for an application. It takes two to three weeks to receive a Social Security number.

PAYING TAXES *The main reason you need a Social Security number is to identify yourself when you pay taxes. What, you may ask, are taxes? Taxes are the money the government collects from people and businesses when they earn money or make a profit. Cities, states, and the federal government all need to raise money— through taxes—to pay for the services they provide, as well as for schools, libraries, some hospitals, roads and bridges, and for the armed forces.*

Just like you, the government makes a budget so that it knows how much money it needs to run the country and, therefore, how much it needs to collect in taxes. The more the government needs, the more it collects. And, the more you earn, the more money you have to pay in taxes. In 1991, anyone who made $400 or more from a business had to pay self-employment taxes and fill out a tax form. No exceptions. Most children will not earn that much money until they get regular jobs, but the minimum tax requirements and the amount you have to pay (the tax rate) change from time to time. To find out how much you might owe, you can talk to your family's accountant or call the <u>Internal Revenue Service (IRS)</u>. The IRS is the government agency that collects federal income tax, which is due on April 15 every year for money earned the year before. Call the IRS Taxpayer Service at 800-829-1040 if you have questions about federal taxes.

On top of federal income taxes, you may also owe state or local income taxes. Some states do not have income taxes, so you will have to check the rules for your area. The agency that collects state and local taxes varies from state to state, too. In California, it is called the State of California Franchise Tax Board, but in your state it may be called something else. You can contact your local **Small Business Administration** or **Chamber of Commerce** to get local tax information, as well as the name of the agency that collects those taxes.

At tax time, lots of people use an accountant to figure out how much tax they must pay and to fill out their tax returns. That's okay, but as a biz kid, you really should learn how to do it yourself. Assuming you have kept good **records** all year, it is not that hard.

Good records prove what your expenses are. You only get taxed on your profits (what the IRS calls **net earnings**). Net earnings are your revenues (the money you take in from customers) minus expenses. You cannot include your own labor as a business expense, but all other expenses count—things like advertising, transportation, and the **cost of goods sold**.

For example, let's say you had a phenomenal year with your lemonade stand and your sales brought you $1,000. The IRS says you have to pay taxes if you had net earnings of at least $400. Does that mean you have to pay taxes? Not necessarily. Why not? Because you forgot to subtract your costs. All those lemons and paper cups must have cost you something. Let's say that the lemons, sugar, and paper cups cost $700, the pitcher cost $30, advertising fliers cost $25, and the yard sign was $10. Add them all up, and your total expenses were $765. Subtract your expenses from your **revenues** and you get your net earnings ($1,000 minus $765 = $235). As far as the IRS is concerned, your business did not make enough profit to be taxed.

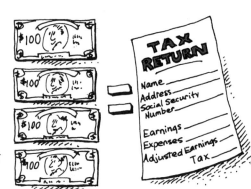

Now can you see why a good record-keeping system is important? Without **receipts** or canceled checks that prove you had those expenses, you might have to pay taxes. On net earnings of $1,000, the tax would be about $280. Ouch, that hurts! But do not ignore your tax obligation because ignoring it is against the law. (That's right, ignorance is no excuse.) If you fail to report net earnings of $400 or more, you might have to pay a penalty, be marked for the rest of your life if the IRS charges you with the crime of tax evasion and you are convicted. Well-kept records are your only defense. Review Chapters Four and Five for suggestions on how to keep track of your money.

If you have questions about tax or business recordkeeping, the IRS is there to help you. And their service is free. You can use the IRS hotline (1-800-829-1040), or, better yet, go to any local IRS office and meet with an IRS representative. No question is too stupid or too trivial. The IRS also has several free booklets to help you, such as Publication #334, *Tax Guide for Small Business.* To order IRS forms or booklets, call the IRS at 1-800-829-3676. Keep in mind that tax rules, rates, and forms change every year, so make sure you get the most recent information.

If you sell a product—as opposed to a service like washing cars—you may have to worry about another type of tax, called a retail **sales tax.** Most states, and some cities, require businesses to

charge their customers a certain percentage of the cost of the item sold (the sales tax) and then pay it to the government. In order to collect sales tax from customers, you must have a license, and you must keep careful records of all your sales. But rules vary from city to city and state to state, so check with your local Small Business Administration, Chamber of Commerce, and your city hall to see whether you must register for a sales tax permit and where you get the necessary form.

LICENSES AND PERMITS   When you talk to the people at city hall, find out if there are other business licenses or permits you must get. For example, some towns require people who sell things to eat to get a food-and-beverage license. You may not need a license to run a lemonade stand or sell cookies or candy door-to-door, but it is a good idea to check it. You want to make sure you are not going to do anything illegal.

Before Brandon started his flower subscription business, he and his Dad went to the county courthouse to find out the local laws. And it's a good thing they did. It turned out Brandon had to register his business name, "Bloomin' Express," and address with the county clerk, and he needed a peddler's license. The county registration makes sure no one else is operating with the same business name in your county. Also, if customers complain to the government because they believe you broke the law or cheated them out of their money, the local authorities can track you down. Each county's requirements are different. Check with your county clerk. Normally, registration costs less than $10. Include the costs of all permits and licenses when you figure out how much to charge your customers.

Most of these laws are intended to regulate bigger enterprises, not kid-sized businesses. But, even though you are "just a kid," pleading ignorance of the law is never an excuse to avoid taxes. And you could be fined for not having the proper permits or licenses. So, learn the laws for your area. Then, live and work by them.

CHAPTER 8

Going Out of Business

BIZ KIDS

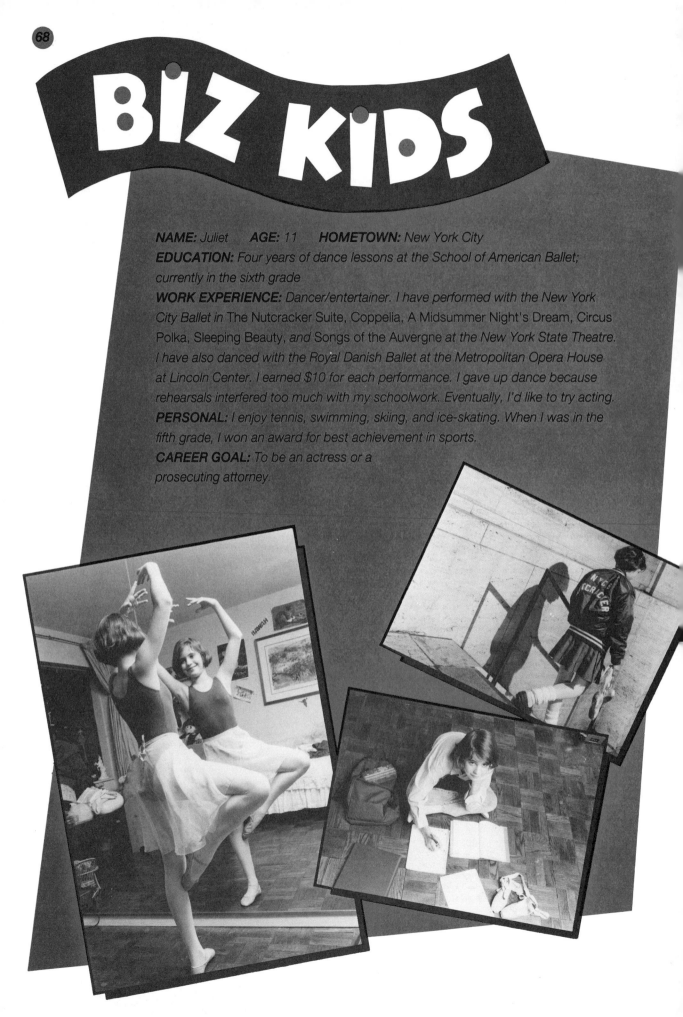

NAME: Juliet   **AGE:** 11   **HOMETOWN:** New York City

EDUCATION: Four years of dance lessons at the School of American Ballet; currently in the sixth grade

WORK EXPERIENCE: Dancer/entertainer. I have performed with the New York City Ballet in The Nutcracker Suite, Coppelia, A Midsummer Night's Dream, Circus Polka, Sleeping Beauty, and Songs of the Auvergne at the New York State Theatre. I have also danced with the Royal Danish Ballet at the Metropolitan Opera House at Lincoln Center. I earned $10 for each performance. I gave up dance because rehearsals interfered too much with my schoolwork. Eventually, I'd like to try acting.

PERSONAL: I enjoy tennis, swimming, skiing, and ice-skating. When I was in the fifth grade, I won an award for best achievement in sports.

CAREER GOAL: To be an actress or a prosecuting attorney.

CHAPTER 8
Going Out of Business

As people get older and more educated, their interests change—and so do their ideas about making money. When Juliet was seven, all she thought about was dancing. So, she went to ballet school to become the best ballerina she could. Juliet got to be so good that she got a part in the New York State Theatre's production of <u>The Nutcracker Suite</u>. Each time she performed, she earned $10. In just one season, she made $200, and she was in the show four seasons in a row. Then, at age eleven, Juliet was not so pleased with her dancing career.

"I just got bored with it," said Juliet, "plus all the rehearsals and dance classes were interfering with my school work."

So, what did Juliet do? What every sensible working person does when a change is needed: she quit.

Quitting does not always mean failing. It can be a way to end one thing to begin something else. In Juliet's case, she gave up dance to concentrate on math—her favorite subject in the sixth grade—and sports, especially softball, soccer, and ice-skating.

She is contemplating becoming a professional ice skater, because, as she said, "I like to be on stage a lot."

Of course, figure skating is as much a performing art as it is a sport, and good skaters can make a lot of money. The truth is, changing careers is common. The average American beginning his or her career in the 1990s probably will work in ten or more jobs for five or more employers before retiring, according to a study by management consultants A.T. Kearney Inc.

Even successful biz kids may tire of their work and decide to do something else. Or maybe you are going away to school or your family has to move and you have to close down your business. Well, consider this: if you have built your business into a fairly good operation, someone will pay you for it. It could just be the biggest sale you ever made. Putting your business up for sale requires all the biz skills you have already learned—from marketing to financial accounting.

ADVERTISE FOR BUYERS   *To begin with, you have to find a buyer. And how do you find a buyer? By advertising, of course. Advertise in all the places you have advertised your product or service, including the various bulletin boards around town. And put an ad in the classified section of the newspaper. Do not forget the value of word-of-mouth advertising. Talk to friends, family, and your neighbors to get them to spread the word. Ask your customers whether they know of someone who would like to take over your business. But this should be a last resort, since you do not want your customers getting worried that you are defecting.*

TARGET BUYERS   *Think about who your most likely buyers are. How about a younger brother or sister or neighborhood kid who has watched and admired you? Or how about competitors who would love to get you out of their hair and pick up your steady customers?*

  *Often a young company's best bait is its future—its potential for greater achievements and growing earnings. Illustrate your company's future in a brochure to hand out to possible buyers. Your brochure can highlight how your business is unique, and how, based on past successes, it is likely to succeed in the future. Show how your company can expand into new markets, beat out competitors, invent, develop, or manufacture new products, revolutionize a service, or produce larger volumes at less cost. Show where expenses will diminish, **debts** will be paid off, and profits will pile up. Just as you did in your business plan, put your best projections for your company on paper in convincing detail.*

NEGOTIATE   *It is tempting to jump at the first offer that comes along, but the time to accept an offer is only after establishing a realistic asking price. When a potential buyer asks, "How much do you want for your business?," you don't want to respond with a wimpy, "Gee, I don't know. What do you think it's worth?" You need a pretty good idea of its value before you look for a buyer. But, keep in mind the difference between value and price. Value is perception of worth; price is what you agree to sell or buy for. Finding the price* *that satisfies both buyer and seller is the most difficult part of the* **valuation** *process.*

To illustrate this point, Arnold Goldstein, author of <u>The Complete Guide to Buying and Selling a Business</u> (John Wiley & Sons, Inc., New York, 1983), tells the story of a kid named Marvin who sat next to him in the second grade.

One day the teacher asked Marvin, "How much is 2 plus 2?"

"It all depends," said Marvin.

"What do you mean it depends?" the teacher shouted.

"It depends on whether I'm buying or selling," he casually replied.

Good old Marvin obviously knew "value" even in the second grade. He used to sell the right answers to the math homework at exorbitant prices. If someone bargained with him for a lower price, Marvin gave him the wrong answers. Years later he was the millionaire owner of a chain of motels and country clubs.

The **bottom line** is, there is no "right" price or special formula that will give you the magic number. For a service type business, your most valuable **assets** are your customers and their continuing need for the service. For a product business, your **inventories** of the product and raw materials may hold the most value for a prospective buyer. But the company's ability to make profits is the most important variable. When negotiating price with a buyer, a good rule is to ask for a year's profit plus the cost of any materials and tools or equipment that are part of the business.

PROVE YOUR PROFITS So, how do you prove to a potential buyer what your profits were last year? You show him or her your financial records. Profits, as you recall, are all your income from customers minus all your expenses. It is the number you reported on your tax return to the IRS. If a buyer is serious about your business, he or she will want to see all your records, including your tax return, your monthly or annual Profit and Loss Statements, all your invoices and receipts, and maybe even your **bank statement**. To prove the value of your assets—things like a lawn mower or a bicycle that are part of the business—you will have to show a sales receipt. Now you will be glad you kept your records up to date. If you didn't, you may have trouble getting the price you want for your business.

By the way, do not even think about coming up with phony numbers. Doctoring your financial statements may be hazardous to your wealth. When you recalculate expenses to beef up profits for past years, the IRS may get into the act, **audit** *you, and make you pay taxes on those supposed profits. In the worst case, the IRS can charge you interest and penalties or even call you a crook and take you to court.*

After the potential buyer has looked over your business, checked out your inventories, and combed through your financial records, you can start negotiating the price. Again, start by asking for one year's profits plus the cost of materials and equipment. If your buyer agrees to your price, lock up the deal. If not, you may have to compromise and come down a bit or look for another buyer.

Once a buyer is hooked, you have to negotiate payment terms and write up a sales contract. Sometimes a buyer cannot afford to pay the entire amount at once. In that case, you may have to take a **note**—*the buyer's promise to pay so much each month over a period of time. You are, in fact, lending the buyer money, which means you can charge interest on the unpaid balance. Make sure the contract has a rule that says if the buyer cannot continue to make payments, you have the right to take back the business or the equipment. You might even ask for collateral to protect yourself against loss of the money that is due.*

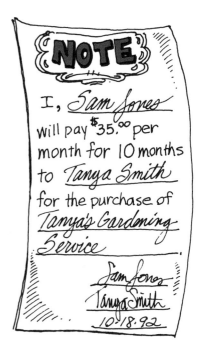

FINANCE THE BUYER *If the buyer cannot pay the entire price in cash, you have the right to check out the buyer's ability to run a business. After all, if the buyer cannot make a profit, he or she probably will not be able to pay you off. Under a new owner, the business may flounder or fail, leaving you with nothing or having to take back the business. To keep a sale from backfiring, carefully screen your buyer for both financial and management ability. Ask questions to determine the buyer's business experience. When prospective buyers ask you for financial information, you can request the same data from them.*

Of course, going out of business does not mean you have to sell it. You could simply quit. But, if you have built a business from scratch and you have found someone who can take it over and run it as efficiently as you have, why not keep it running? And why not take the reward for all the hard work you put into it?

Since many buyers want sellers to stay on for a while to keep things running smoothly while they learn the ropes, you may be able to work out a special deal for yourself. Assuming, of course, that you can adapt to being an **employee**, you might negotiate more for yourself in an **employment contract**. If the new owner does not ask you to work for the company, you may be restricted by an agreement not to compete—your promise not to engage in the same business for a period of time. For many a hard-core biz kid, an agreement not to compete may be harder to live with than the decision to sell out.

CHAPTER

9

For Further Information

BIZ KIDS

NAME: Gerald   **AGE:** 16   **HOMETOWN:** Philadelphia
EDUCATION: High school student
WORK EXPERIENCE: I design and sell silk-screened T-shirts. In the summer before my junior year of high school, I attended a two-week seminar for young entrepreneurs at the Wharton Business School. That's where I learned about marketing, production, and finance. I put together a business plan, and took it to a man I met at the seminar who helped me get a $1,000 grant to start my T-shirt business. By buying T-shirts in bulk, my cost is $2.50 per shirt; I put my design on the shirts and charge $10 apiece. I advertise my business with fliers, and I sell most of my merchandise to students in my school.
PERSONAL: I enjoy sports, mainly basketball.
CAREER GOAL: To start a business manufacturing and selling an entire line of sportswear after college.

CHAPTER 9
For Further Information

As you start in business, and continue to grow, you will have plenty of questions. Luckily, many resources, including organizations, books, periodicals and people, can help you. Here are a few of the best.

General Organizations.

Small Business Administration (SBA): A federal agency that assists businesses with less than 100 employees. More than 140 publications are available at SBA district offices or write to the SBA distribution center, P.O. Box 30, Denver, CO 80201-0030. Call 1-800-827-5722 for the nearest SBA office and The Small Business Answer Desk, which helps with specific questions.

SCORE/ACE: The Service Corps of Retired Executives (SCORE) and the Active Corps of Executives (ACE) are SBA volunteer programs. SCORE and ACE volunteers provide counseling and workshops and seminars for small businesses. Call your local SCORE or SBA office for a counseling application.

Small Business Development Centers (SBDC): University-based centers providing free individual counseling and practical training for small businesses. Call the SBA at 1-800-827-5722 for the nearest SBDC.

These are also excellent resources:

Chamber of Commerce of the United States, 1615 H Street NW, Washington D.C. 20062. 202-659-6000. (Also call your local and state chambers.)

Consumer Information Center, P.O. Box 100, Pueblo, CO 81002. (Ask for the free catalog.)

Department of Commerce, 14th Street NW, Washington, D.C. 20230. 202-377-1472.

Internal Revenue Service. Call your local IRS office or 1-800-829-1040.

National Federation of Independent Business, 600 Maryland Ave. SW, Suite 700, Washington D.C. 20024. 202-554-9000.

Organizations for Young People. *There are also groups specifically for biz-minded kids. Check out:*

Center for Entrepreneurship: *Has tips for pre-teens, teens, and college students. Write the Center at Wichita State University, Wichita, KS 67208.*

Distributive Education Clubs of America (DECA): *A student-centered organization with leadership and personal development programs offered by state departments of education, with chapters in every state. Write to DECA's Executive Director at 1908 Association Drive, Reston, VA 22091 or call 703-860-5000.*

Future Business Leaders of America: *Assists high school students. Call 703-860-3334 for membership information and competition details.*

Junior Achievement (JA): *Offers "Business Basics" for fifth and sixth graders and "Project Business" for junior-high students. Write 5 Landmark Square, Stamford, CT 06901 or call 203-327-2535.*

National 4-H Council: *Write for the Learn to Earn program, 7100 Connecticut Avenue, Chevy Chase, MD 20815.*

Organizations Offering Legal or Financial Advice:

Accounting: *Referrals through local accountants' associations, chambers of commerce, the Yellow Pages, or recommendations of other small businesses.*

Business license/permit: *A legal authorization in document form that may be required to run a business. Contact city hall, county court, state small business program office, or SBA district office for assistance.*

Business name: *Businesses must register a business name, usually on a "doing business as" (D.B.A.) form, with the local government. This prevents any other business from using the same name for a similar business in the same area. Get a form from the county clerk.*

Copyright: *Gives the owner the exclusive right to copy the work for publication and sale. Copyrights for works of art, sculpture,*

COPYRIGHT

music and published or unpublished manuscripts should be registered with the Copyright Office of the Library of Congress. Call 202-707-9100.

Patent: A copyright for inventors. Inventors should contact the Patent Office of the Department of Commerce. Special publications are available from the SBA. Or call the Patent Office, 703-557-3158.

Trademark: A distinctive mark or emblem stamped on a product that allows that product to be identified in the market. Trademarks should be registered with the Trademark Office of the Department of Commerce, 703-308-9000.

Taxes: Order the Internal Revenue Service Tax Guide for Small Business (publication #334), 800-829-3676. For tax-related questions, call 800-829-1040 or go to any local IRS office.

Publications. Consumers Union's <u>Zillions</u>, bi-monthly magazine for eight- to fourteen-year-olds, teaches kids about money. Other periodicals are at newsstands and libraries.

Camps and Competitions.:

Dollars & Sense Financial Camp, run by Smart Services Inc., of West Palm Beach, Florida. Five-day programs and weekend workshops on money management. 407-655-2229.

Exchange City, Kansas City, Missouri. Camp set in a mock-up of a town square. Kids run their own community. 816-234-9177.

Outstanding Young Business Owner: A competition open to anyone who owned a business by age twenty-one and can document success. Top prize $1,000. National Federation of Independent Business, 600 Maryland Avenue S.W., Washington, D.C. 20024.

Young Americans Success Camp, Jefferson Institute. Fourteen-day trip to Russia teaches kids to set up and manage their own businesses. 800-672-6019.

SOME SIMPLE EXERCISES *Do you have what it takes to be an entrepreneur? Circle TRUE or FALSE to the following:*

If you say most of these are true, then chances are you have the energy and motivation to be a successful biz kid.

I am a risk-taker. I like to take chances.	T or F
I love to learn and I like school.	T or F
I am independent and like to make my own decisions.	T or F
I am impatient and get bored easily.	T or F
I hate to waste time sleeping. I don't need much sleep.	T or F
When I do things I like, I have a lot of energy.	T or F
I always finish what I start.	T or F
I know how to plan and set goals.	T or F
I never worry about what other people think about me.	T or F
It is pretty easy to get others to do things for me.	T or F
Sometimes I do things just to prove I can do them.	T or F
I am constantly thinking up new ideas.	T or F

CHECKLIST FOR STARTING A BUSINESS   *These are the questions you face when starting a business. Check off each question on this SBA list to which you can answer yes.*

Also, talk to a local entrepreneur. Ask him or her: Where did you get the idea for your business? What's your market area? What is important about your customers? What's your competition?

___Do you want your own business badly enough to work long hours without knowing how much money you will end up with?

___Do you know how much money you will need to get your business started?

___Have you figured out how much money of your own you can put into the business?

___Do you know where you can borrow the rest of the money you may need to start your business?

___Have you figured out the annual income you expect to get from the business?

___Do you know what kind of customers will want to buy your product or service?

___Are there enough customers of this kind in your area?

___Have you found a good location for your business?

___Do you have an idea of what the equipment and supplies will cost?

___Can you save money by buying second-hand equipment or leasing rather than buying?

___Have you found suppliers who will sell you merchandise at a good price?

___Have you compared the prices of different suppliers?

___Have you worked out a record-keeping system to keep track of your business income and expenses—what you owe people and what they owe you?

___Do you know what financial statements you will need to prepare and how to use them?

___Do you know an accountant who will help with your records and financial statements?

___Do you have your Social Security number?

___Do you know what licenses and permits you need?

___Have you decided how you will market or advertise your business?

___Do you know how to figure what you should charge your customers?

___Do you know what your competitors charge for goods or services like yours?

___Will the price you charge allow you to make a profit?

___Do you have a work schedule (how many hours you will work each week or month)?

___Does your family support your plan to start a business of your own?

EASY-TO-USE BUSINESS FORMS AND WORKSHEETS

Use this six-step worksheet to develop your own business plan.

STEP NUMBER ONE: *My Business Goals*

I hope to earn $_____ every (week/month/year)

I want to make enough money to buy _____

by _____ (date) or save for _____

STEP NUMBER TWO: *What Is My Business*

The name of my business is _____

My service or product is _____

It will be better or different from my competitors' because _____

_____

What makes my business the best is _____

My business is located _____

The kind of customers attracted to my business are _____

_____

STEP NUMBER THREE: *My Timetable*

I plan to start my business on _____ (month/year)

I will stay in business for _____ (weeks/months/years)

I can work on my business at the times below:

   MON.   TUES.   WED.   THURS.   FRI.   SAT.   SUN.

Time during day _____

# of hours per day _____

I can work a total of _____ hours each week.

STEP NUMBER FOUR: *My Costs*

Business costs are two types: fixed and variable. Fixed costs are unrelated to the number of customers; they include materials and equipment needed to run day-to-day business operations. Fixed costs include start-up expenses: office supplies, equipment, telephone installation, an answering machine, or a desk. During the course of running your business, other ongoing fixed costs include advertising, telephone bills, and office supplies.

My fixed costs will be:

Start-up expenses		Other fixed expenses (estimate a monthly amount)	
Item	Cost	Item	Cost
_____	$_____	_____	$_____
_____	_____	_____	_____
_____	_____	_____	_____
Total start-up costs:	$_____	Total other fixed costs:	$_____

Variable costs vary depending upon the number of products you sell or the number of customers.

My variable costs per product or per customer will be:

Item	Cost
_____	$_____
_____	_____
_____	_____
Total variable costs:	$_____

STEP NUMBER FIVE: *My Prices*

In establishing prices, entrepreneurs should call the competition to see what they charge. Because you are new, inexperienced, and want to build a business fast, you may have to set prices significantly lower than your competition. If you cannot afford to charge 25 to 30 percent less than your professional, established competitors, consider another business. Follow these steps to arrive at a price:

A: I want to earn at least $_____ per hour.

B: It takes me _____ hours per product or customer

C: My total fixed and variable costs per product or service are

$_____

Now multiply your hourly wage (A) by your time estimate (B), then add in your variable costs (C) to bring you to a total price.

(A)   _____ hours per customer

X

(B) $_____ per hour

+

(C) $_____ (total costs)

=

$_____ (final price)

STEP NUMBER SIX: *Will I Make a Profit?*

The final step is estimating how much business you expect and what your profits will be. From what you know of your market, estimate the number of customers you will service or products you will sell each month, and calculate your profits.

	# of customers	x	price per customer	=	total income	−	cost per customer	=	Profit (Loss)
Jan		x		=		−		=	
Feb		x		=		−		=	
Mar		x		=		−		=	
Apr		x		=		−		=	
May		x		=		−		=	
June		x		=		−		=	
July		x		=		−		=	
Aug		x		=		−		=	
Sept		x		=		−		=	
Oct		x		=		−		=	
Nov		x		=		−		=	
Dec		x		=		−		=	

Total Income − Total Costs = Profit/(Loss)

MONTHLY BUDGET

List all possible income   Amounts

_____ $_____

List all possible expenses

_____ $_____

Total income = _____   Total expenses = _____

BOOKKEEPING RECORD *You need to keep good records of income and expenses so when it's time to pay taxes you pay tax only on your profits (income minus expenses). Your record-keeping system can be simple or elaborate. Buy an appointment book and business planner from an office supplies store or simply keep track in a spiral notebook of the money you spend, the money you take in, and the time you work. Make a copy of the following for each month:*

MONTHLY BOOKKEEPING RECORD FOR THE MONTH OF _____

Date	Check No./ Invoice No.	To whom paid/ from whom collected	Description	Income	Amount Expense
_____	_____	_____	_____	$_____	$_____
_____	_____	_____	_____	$_____	$_____
_____	_____	_____	_____	$_____	$_____
_____	_____	_____	_____	$_____	$_____
_____	_____	_____	_____	$_____	$_____
_____	_____	_____	_____	$_____	$_____
_____	_____	_____	_____	$_____	$_____
_____	_____	_____	_____	$_____	$_____
_____	_____	_____	_____	$_____	$_____
_____	_____	_____	_____	$_____	$_____
			TOTAL FOR THE MONTH	$_____	$_____

PROFIT and LOSS STATEMENT *At the end of each month, subtract the expenses you had during that time period from your income to calculate whether you had a profit (you made money) or loss (you lost money).*

PROFIT and LOSS STATEMENT FOR MONTH OF _____

Total Income: _____

minus Total Expenses: _____

= PROFIT (or LOSS): _____

INVOICE FORMS: INCOME AND EXPENSE RECEIPTS

Keep the sales receipts for merchandise, supplies, or equipment you buy as evidence of expenses. If you pay by check, your canceled check is another expense receipt. To keep track of income, each time you sell something or do a job, fill out an invoice (customer receipt). Use carbon paper to make copies for you and your customer.

INVOICE	
Date: _____	Invoice No.: _____
Customer: _____	
Address: _____	
_____	

Money received for:	Amount:
_____	$_____
_____	$_____
_____	$_____
_____	$_____
_____	$_____
_____	$_____
_____	$_____
_____	$_____
_____	$_____
_____	$_____
Subtotal	$_____
Tax	$_____
TOTAL PAID	$_____

LOAN DOCUMENT

This document certifies that I,

_____ ,

have borrowed the sum of $_____

from _____ .

The loan is for a period of _____ (weeks/months/years).

Payments are due on the _____ of every _____ .

The first payment is due on _____ and the last payment is due on _____ .

This loan carries an interest rate of _____ % per _____ .

Payments are to be in equal installments of $_____ .

Total number of payments shall be _____ .

I agree to pay an additional $_____ as a late penalty if I miss the payment schedule by more than five days.

Borrower's signature _____

Lender's signature _____

Date _____

Glossary:

A LIST OF BIZ WORDS YOU SHOULD KNOW AND UNDERSTAND

accounting: organizing financial transactions. Includes budgeting, financial reporting, and tax preparation.

advertising: paid forms of publicity announcing or attracting attention to business. Usually found in television, radio, magazines, and newspapers.

asset: anything of lasting value to a person or business, such as money, equipment, and materials. Assets can be repossessed when loans are not repaid.

audit: IRS examination of your tax return, generally limited to three-years after filing.

balancing the budget: making sure amount spent is not more than the amount received.

balance sheet: listing of all assets (what you own) and all liabilities (what you owe). Liabilities subtracted from assets is net worth.

bank statement: record of deposits, withdrawals, fees charged, and interest earned on a bank account.

bookkeeping: recording of financial transactions.

bottom line: amount of profit or loss.

break-even: when sources of income exactly equal expenses and the bottom line is zero.

brochure: small booklet or advertising sheet folded into a booklet.

budget: plan of how much to spend and how it will be spent.

business concept: brief description of a business and what makes it uniquely better than the competition.

business plan: written statement of how a new business will start. Usually describes product or service; estimates costs, prices and profits, and lists short- and long-range goals.

capital: money used to run a business to pay for inventory, equipment, and other expenses. Most start-up capital comes from the entrepreneur, family, and friends.

career: profession for which one trains; the way one earns a living.

Chamber of Commerce: non-profit organization promoting American business and helping businesses.

check: written order to a bank to pay a specified amount of money to a person or company from money on deposit.

checking account: bank account from which you write checks drawing on deposits.

child labor laws: federal and state laws protecting children from being hurt or overworked.

closing: end of a sales pitch; asking for the customer's business.

collateral: asset or property that a borrower owns and promises to give a lender in case of default on a loan.

competition: companies with similar products or services trying to get the same customers.

consumer: person who buys goods or services; a customer.

cost of goods sold: expenses a business incurs to manufacture or buy the product or perform the service it sells.

credit: money loaned that may be repaid in the future, usually for a fee.

customer: person who buys goods or services; a consumer.

customer service: responsibility to give customers what they want. Many successful companies name customer service as the main reason for success.

debt: money you owe when you buy on credit or borrow.

default: fail to pay back a loan on its original terms.

demand: desire for a product or service; amount people are ready and able to buy at a certain price.

dependable: *trusted, to be relied on.*

deposit: *place in a bank.*

direct mail: *advertising in which letters or brochures are mailed directly to potential customers.*

donate: *give to good cause or charity.*

door-to-door: *going from home to home to tell people about a service or to sell a product.*

down payment: *partial payment toward a purchase, with full payment to come later.*

due diligence: *thorough examination of a company.*

earn-out: *agreement in which seller earns part of the purchase price or bonus from company's future profits.*

earnings: *profits; the amount by which revenues exceed expenses.*

economics: *science that studies matters related to money and production, distribution, sale, and use of goods and services.*

economy: *the flow of money in a society.*

employ: *hire for pay.*

employees: *people who work for a business owner.*

employment contract: *agreement committing a seller to work for a buyer in the acquired company.*

entrepreneur: *one who starts, manages, and assumes the risks of a business. Entrepreneurs uncover problems affecting a large number of people, and organize businesses to deliver solutions.*

entrepreneurship: *assuming the risks of owning a business.*

expand: *grow bigger; to enlarge.*

expense: *a cost of doing business.*

Fair Labor Standards Act: *federal law governing employment practices and the hiring of children.*

fee: *charge for a service.*

FICA: *Federal Insurance Contributions Act. Social Security*

tax, which you pay based on earnings is paid back in monthly installments when you retire.

finance: *area of business dealing with money, banking, and investments.*

financials: *formal document stating company's financial results.*

finished goods: *manufactured product.*

fixed costs: *regular, ongoing costs of running a business not dependent on number of customers.*

fliers: *sheets of paper printed with advertising, usually the best forms of advertising for biz kids. Can be distributed door-to-door or on car windshields.*

garage sale: *sale of used items at bargain prices.*

gift certificate: *written statement traded for a service or product. Usually bought to be given as a present.*

goal: *set of desired outcomes; target.*

going rate: *amount of money most often paid for a certain job.*

guarantee: *promise or agreement stating the quality or length of time a product or service should last.*

income: *money received from customers through the sale of products or services.*

income statement: *financial statement showing profit earned over a period of time. Also called Profit and Loss Statement.*

income tax: *fee charged by state and federal governments based on a percentage of your income.*

innovation: *something new and different.*

interest: *fee paid for the use of borrowed money or what a bank pays for the money you have deposited.*

Internal Revenue Service (IRS): *federal agency that collects taxes.*

inventory: supplies, materials, or products on hand to be sold. A supply of product.

investment: use of money to produce income or profit.

invoice: statement issued to customers to record a sale. One copy is the customer's and one is the seller's.

IOU: stands for "I owe you"; see loan document.

lending officer: banker who negotiates loans.

liability: a debt owed.

loan: money borrowed for a certain period of time to be paid back at a certain interest rate, usually in installments.

loan document: IOU or written agreement describing loan agreement. Names the amount borrowed and payback schedule. Signed by the borrower and lender.

loss: amount by which the costs of a business (expenses) are greater than the sales (income).

management: leadership and guidance of a business.

market: specific category of potential buyers.

market research: finding out what customers want.

marketing: getting the right goods and services to the right people at the right price by promoting and advertising.

merchandise: goods that someone wants to sell.

net earnings: profits before taxes are paid.

net worth: total assets minus total liabilities. Derived by subtracting the value of everything you owe from everything you own.

note: written promise to repay a loan.

newsletter: small newspaper for and about a certain group of people.

outgo: money paid out; expenses.

overhead: fixed costs of doing business.

pamphlet: thin booklet.

passbook savings account: bank account that pays interest on deposits.

patent: right to a process or a product granted to inventor.

plan: list of steps taken in order to reach a goal.

power words: words that set off a positive emotional response in a customer toward your product or service.

press release: document sent to the media describing a newsworthy event.

price list: list of the amounts you are asking to be paid.

principal: original amount of money loaned before interest has been added.

priorities: most important things that need to be done.

product: what you make, find, or buy that can be sold for profit.

profit: amount of money left after paying expenses. (Compare to "loss".) Profit equals income minus expenses.

Profit and Loss Statement: same as income statement. Summarizes the income and expenses of a company to show the profit or loss for a specific period of time.

proprietor: owner of a business.

prospect: potential customer.

prototype: model for a product.

public relations: art of getting people to understand and like something, such as a business or product.

purchase agreement: legal agreement between buyer and seller describing terms for the sale of a company.

raw materials: materials used to produce finished goods.

recommend: praise or to speak well of someone.

receipt: record of funds received.

Sonia's Sewing Service

OVERHEAD:
PER MONTH

sewing machine $35.00
cutting table 18.00
mannequin 15.00
fabric 42.00
pins, buttons 8.00

records: *written accounts to be saved for future use.*

refund: *money given back to a dissatisfied customer.*

resumé: *short account of one's work experience and qualifications.*

revenue: *money a business receives in payment for products or services sold.*

risk: *take a chance.*

salary: *annual earnings of an employee.*

sales pitch: *snappy, verbal description of product or service being sold.*

sales tax: *fee charged by most state and some city governments based on a percentage of the selling price of a product.*

satisfied customer: *client happy with a purchased product or service.*

savings: *money put in a safe place so that it can be used later.*

schedule: *time plan.*

self-employed: *working for yourself.*

service: *work done for others.*

slogan: *motto or phrase used to describe product or service and to get the attention of potential customers.*

Small Business Administration: *agency of the United States Department of Commerce that assists entrepreneurs.*

Social Security Tax: *collected by the federal government to pay benefits to workers when they retire (see FICA).*

sole proprietorship: *business owned by one person.*

start-up costs: *expenses of setting up a new business.*

supplier: *business that sells items to another business.*

supply: *amount of finished goods available for purchase.*

target customers: *people or consumers most likely to want or need your service or product.*

tax identification number: *your Social Security number.*

valuation: *formal process of determining company's worth.*

variable costs: *expenses that rise or fall based on the number of customers served or products sold.*

venture: *business undertaking.*

wages: *per-hour earnings of employees.*

wholesale: *sales of goods or services by one business to another.*

withdrawal: *removal of money from a bank account.*

zoning: *local government regulation of where and how small businesses can be run.*

NOTE TO READER:

If this book has not answered all your questions, please write to me:
Terri Thompson
% Barron's Educational Series, Inc.
250 Wireless Boulevard
Hauppauge, NY 11788